The Road to Renewal

The Road to Renewal

Private Investment in U.S.
Transportation Infrastructure

R. Richard Geddes

The AEI Press

Publisher for the American Enterprise Institute

WASHINGTON, D.C.

Distributed by arrangement with the Rowman & Littlefield Publishing Group, 4501 Forbes Boulevard, Suite 200, Lanham, Maryland 20706. To order, call toll free 1-800-462-6420 or 1-717-794-3800. For all other inquiries, please contact AEI Press, 1150 Seventeenth Street, N.W., Washington, D.C. 20036, or call 1-800-862-5801.

Library of Congress Cataloging-in-Publication Data

Geddes, R. Richard.
  The road to renewal: private investment in U.S. transportation
infrastructure / R. Richard Geddes.
      p. cm.
  Includes bibliographical references and index.
  ISBN-13: 978-0-8447-4346-2 (cloth)
  ISBN-10: 0-8447-4346-1 (cloth)
  ISBN-13: 978-0-8447-4347-9 (pbk.)
  ISBN-10: 0-8447-4347-X (pbk.)
  [etc.]
  1. Transportation—United States—Finance. 2. Transportation engineering—
United States—Finance. 3. Infrastructure (Economics)—United States—
Finance. 4. Public-private sector cooperation—United States. I. Title.

  HE206.2.G43 2010
  388'.049—dc22

Printed in the United States of America

Contents

List of Illustrations

Acknowledgments

I am grateful to many people for their assistance in the preparation of this book. I have benefited from discussions with and suggestions from Germà Bel, Ross Bevevino, Susan Binder, Shane Chalke, Tyler Duvall, John Foote, Joe Giglio, D. J. Gribbon, Amy Hawkins, Ken Orski, Jeff Shane, and Clifford Winston. I also learned much from lively discussion and debate with fellow members of the National Surface Transportation Policy and Revenue Study Commission: Frank Busalacchi, Maria Cino, Steve Heminger, Frank McArdle, Secretary Norman Mineta, Steve Odland, Secretary Mary Peters, Patrick Quinn, Matt Rose, Jack Schenendorf, Tom Skancke, and the late Paul Weyrich. I am indebted to all the staff of the U.S. Department of Transportation who assisted the commission with its work and thus laid the groundwork for many concepts discussed here. Cornell University students Alex Bowerman and Julia Melamud provided excellent research assistance. Emily Batman, Laura Harbold, Henry Olsen, Mary Peters, Bob Poole, Peter Samuel, and three anonymous referees read earlier versions of the book and provided indispensable comments and suggestions. I am thankful to Adrian Moore for help with several technical issues. I am also grateful to the Australian-American Fulbright Commission for its support and encouragement. The Economics Program in the Research School of Social Science, Australian National University, and the Australian government's Productivity Commission were both gracious hosts during the book's completion. Finally, I am grateful to the American Enterprise Institute for its assistance during every stage of this process.

Preface

Large-scale private investment in transportation infrastructure has the potential to thoroughly revitalize America's highway, bridge, tunnel, port, and intermodal systems, which are in desperate need of expansion, renovation, and repair. The dire fiscal condition of many states and localities means that fewer public dollars are available for infrastructure, making private investment especially timely. Private investment not only injects vast amounts of capital into transportation system maintenance and expansion, but also introduces the sharp, focused incentives that are necessary to operate, upgrade, and expand key facilities efficiently.

The principal mechanism for injecting the fresh capital and incentives of private investment into America's transportation system is the public-private partnership, or PPP. "Public-private partnership" has become a catchall phrase for an array of contractual relationships between one or more private parties and a public-sector entity. Transportation PPPs are neither a risky nor an experimental approach. Other countries have been using PPPs of various forms for decades, and in some cases for over a century. The United States itself has extensive experience with this approach. Most of America's early river crossings and bridges and many major roads depended on the grant of a toll charter to private investors. Among the most common companies to issue stock in the first half of the nineteenth century were those that privately financed turnpikes.

Despite their importance, and despite the efforts of a small but growing group of analysts and commentators on their behalf, many misconceptions about PPPs remain. Some stem from an inadequate appreciation of the nature and role of property rights in the transportation sector. For example, some analysis of PPPs proceeds as if U.S. transportation facilities were today essentially unowned, arguing that the exclusion of private investors creates a "savings," since no returns need be paid to equity holders. This ignores the fact that citizens own the vast majority of U.S. transportation facilities and, like any investors, deserve a competitive return on their investment. PPP-induced competition for the use of citizens' capital will improve those returns.

While PPPs are often—and justifiably—promoted for their ability to tap new pools of capital that can be used to renovate existing facilities and construct new ones, and for their ability to assume risk, the effect of private participation on the incentives of facility operators is less well appreciated. Economists are in broad agreement that transportation facilities are precisely the type of assets—those whose contractual performance can be monitored effectively—in which the focused incentives associated with private participation create social benefits such as the rationalization of transportation investments and the provision of information about the true value of transportation facilities. It is thus not only new capital investment and risk assumption, but also the associated high-powered incentives that have the potential to rejuvenate America's beleaguered transportation sector. I explore the effects of those incentives in this book.

Another underappreciated benefit of PPPs is that they inject fresh competition into a range of transportation activities. Competition is a powerful force for promoting social welfare, since it encourages firms to operate efficiently, to focus on customers, and to adopt new technologies rapidly. PPPs already benefit motorists, taxpayers, and investors by allowing competition in several dimensions of transportation provision, such as facility design and construction. In addition to competing for citizen-owners' capital, PPPs can bring competition to new activities, including facility financing, maintenance, expansion, and operation.

Moreover, the PPP approach is often assessed in isolation; potential challenges associated with private investment are considered without reflecting on how those same issues might arise under current practice. One of this book's key themes is that the advantages and disadvantages of PPPs must be assessed within the context of a critical question: "Compared to what?" PPPs are, for example, sometimes charged with creating a loss of public control over critical transportation assets. But control under a PPP approach must be assessed relative to the public's control under a traditional procurement approach. By incorporating detailed, transparent, and enforceable contracts, well-executed PPPs in fact improve public control over transportation facilities.

Many discussions of PPPs focus on the benefits to demanders of capital—the states and localities that desperately need new investment in transportation infrastructure. The benefits to the other side of this market— the debt and equity investors who supply that fresh capital—are often downplayed. Yet PPPs have the potential to expand enormously an important new class of alternative investments in transportation and related infrastructure. Though appealing to many investors, transportation infra- structure is likely to be especially attractive to those already benefiting from tax-exempt status, such as pension funds and nonprofit enterprises. The creation of unique, long-term investment opportunities to improve the retirements of teachers, police, and firemen remains an underappre- ciated social benefit of PPPs.

Some observers also assume that PPPs can only be used on facilities that generate enough toll revenue to make them profitable. That is false. Even if a facility loses money, competitive bidding through PPPs ensures that the public pays the least possible subsidy required to keep it in operation—an approach that has been used in other countries.

But commentators sometimes overlook relevant experience interna- tionally and in related economic sectors. A diverse set of countries— including Australia, Austria, France, Greece, Hungary, Italy, Japan, Poland, Portugal, Spain, the United Kingdom, and many others—is using PPPs in several transportation-related areas. The United States itself has consider- able experience with private investment in many industries that share a similar network structure with transportation, including natural gas, electricity, cable television, railroads, and telecommunications.[1] Many of these industries have been financed through private investment for generations. Underinvestment in any of them would not result in calls for higher taxes to fill the gap, but instead in calls for an environment that would better facilitate private investment.

Moreover, PPPs are now being used in many countries to finance a host of activities loosely termed "social infrastructure." These include the building and management of hospitals, prisons, schools, courthouses, and desalination plants. Insights into issues such as service quality assurance, contractual renegotiation, and the control of market power can be gleaned from international experience with the private financing of both transportation and social infrastructure, as well as America's own experience in network industries.

Part of the solution to America's formidable transportation problems lies in changing the process that directs transportation investment. Another key theme is that the widespread introduction of private investment will dramatically alter the way scarce transportation dollars are allocated. As the numerous earmarks in the 2005 highway reauthorization bill suggest, much of America's federal transportation spending today is directed by political calculations rather than by benefits to motorists and taxpayers in their capacity as investors. The PPP approach allows capital to flow to those investments that transportation customers—motorists—value most highly.[2] Returns on investment are highest on the facilities that motorist-customers use the most, and private participants will seek those returns. Competitively provided capital, taking prudent risks, will result in project choices that are based more on economic value and less on politics.

The stakes could not be higher. Today about 3.9 million miles of public roads and highways traverse the United States, with hundreds of thousands of bridges and tunnels on them. Americans use that system intensively. In 2008, for example, total vehicle miles traveled in the United States exceeded 2.92 trillion.[3] America's transportation system has fostered citizens' mobility, enhanced U.S. competitiveness, and supported the nation's economic growth for decades. Given projected increases in urban and suburban populations, as well as in domestic and international commerce, the importance of our transportation system will continue to grow.

The United States deserves a transportation system befitting a first-world nation. That system should be accountable first and foremost to the citizens who own it. The new U.S. transportation policy approach outlined here creates accountability to citizen-owners but also offers the best possible service to the system's customers—the commuters, vacationers, truckers, delivery companies, and all the others it is meant to serve. That system should be able to move people and goods in a timely, predictable fashion throughout the country, without dilapidated facilities destroying the vehicles that use it.

Risk-taking private capital played a critical role in constructing America's railroads, electric grid, waterworks, and Internet network. It was central to building our road, bridge, and canal systems in the nineteenth century. A vast global supply of capital is ready today to invest in U.S. infrastructure, and the need for that investment is overwhelming. It is time to develop the policy framework to allow private capital to expand and renovate America's surface transportation system in the twenty-first century. In this book, I articulate a new vision for America's surface transportation system that will help achieve this worthy goal.

Introduction

The challenges facing America's transportation system today are unlike any it has ever faced before. The critical problem is no longer funding and constructing a network of high-speed, limited-access interstate highways, as envisioned by President Dwight D. Eisenhower in the Federal-Aid Highway Act of 1956. It is no longer lack of connectivity, between highways or between farms and markets, as it was in the early twentieth century. The U.S. transportation system today faces new and formidable—but surmountable—challenges. They call for a new approach appropriate for a twenty-first-century America.

One major problem is rising traffic congestion. Drivers feel its effects daily, and its economic costs are escalating. The time it takes to travel from one point to another, as well as uncertainty about travel time, is growing. The overall cost of traffic congestion rose almost 400 percent between 1982 and 2003, and its annual cost to the economy stood at over $85 billion in 2008.[1] Congestion not only absorbs motorists' time,[2] but also harms the environment, as vehicle emissions are significantly higher in congested traffic. Almost 3 billion gallons of gasoline are wasted annually as a result.[3] Moreover, the stress and delays associated with congestion have been identified as an important source of discontent.[4] The overall *performance* of America's transportation system—its ability to move people and goods in a smooth, timely, and predictable fashion—has disintegrated.

A second, related problem is weak, inadequate, and deteriorating transportation infrastructure. The United States, an otherwise wealthy nation, has been laboring under the burden of dilapidated transportation infrastructure for far too long. Indeed, the phrase "crumbling infrastructure" with reference to transportation has been an established part of the American lexicon for decades. In 2009, the American Society of Civil

Engineers assigned the nation's roads a grade of D– based on their condition. Bridges received a C and transit a D. The society stated that "the nation is failing to maintain even the current substandard conditions, a dangerous trend that is affecting highway safety and the health of the economy."[5] Similarly, a 2009 study of the condition of America's transportation infrastructure, conducted jointly by the American Association of State Highway and Transportation Officials and the National Transportation Research Group, found that one-third of the country's highways were in poor condition, including over one-fourth of the major urban roads.[6] Appalling and sometimes fatal bridge and tunnel failures are periodic reminders of America's chronically deficient transportation infrastructure.

A third major threat to the system is the rising misdirection and politicization of transportation spending. Federal highway spending in particular is notorious for its lack of direction and its subjection to political influence. Federal earmarks in general and the "bridge to nowhere" in particular have become emblematic of wasteful, unfocused transportation spending, as has political corruption associated with that spending.[7] The growth in transportation earmarks over time is striking. The 1982 highway bill contained only 10 earmarked projects at a cost of $0.36 billion. In 1987, there were 152 earmarked projects at a cost of $1.4 billion. There were 538 earmarks in 1991 at a cost of $6.2 billion, and 1,850 in 1998 at a cost of $9.4 billion. The 2005 highway reauthorization bill contained an astounding 6,371 such earmarks at a total cost of $47 billion.[8]

Earmarks are troubling for several reasons. They circumvent processes that independently assess a project's merit and usually weed out some of the more wasteful cases. Exempt from executive branch review, earmarked projects need not pass any cost-benefit analysis, rigorous or otherwise, and can easily generate costs that are greater than realized benefits. Importantly, projects that generate costs greater than their benefits destroy, rather than create, economic value. A 2007 report by the U.S. Department of Transportation's Office of Inspector General concluded:

> Our review of 7,760 earmarked projects valued at $8.05 billion within [Federal Highway Administration, Federal Transit Administration, and Federal Aviation Administration] programs disclosed that 7,724 of the 7,760 projects (99 percent) either were not

subject to the agencies' review and selection processes or bypassed the states' normal planning and programming processes.[9]

Additionally, the "opportunity cost" of the project is never considered by comparing the intended use of the money to other, perhaps better, uses. Without these important screens and checks, earmarked spending naturally gravitates to politically expedient projects.

Moreover, congressional earmarks often actually harm, rather than help, the transportation system of the state to which they are directed. They divert funds from higher-priority projects and reduce the amount of flexible transportation funds the state receives.[10] For example, Congress allocated $1 billion in federal earmarks to Alaska in the 2005 highway reauthorization bill. That earmarked spending counted against Alaska in determining the total number of federal dollars the state would receive from the fuel-tax revenues it collected, eventually displacing $119 million of state highway projects per year over the authorization period.

Additionally, earmarked spending is usually insufficient to cover a project's cost, forcing the state either to make up the shortfall using its own scarce transportation dollars or to leave funds unspent—even though the state may wish to pursue higher-priority transportation projects. A U.S. Department of Transportation study has shown that a federal earmark covers, on average, only about 10 percent of a project's total cost.[11]

This rising politicization and misdirection of transportation spending also has indirect effects. Unsurprisingly, voters are unwilling to allocate more tax revenue to federal programs when they perceive that those dollars will not be used wisely. Perceived waste in transportation spending has made it politically more difficult to raise fuel taxes; the federal gas tax has not been increased since 1993. Federal spending on transportation has become variable and uncertain, not only subject to political whims but also failing to keep up with inflation.

These three related threats—transportation system performance failure, insufficient investment, and politicization of public transportation spending—pose a serious risk to the U.S. economy at a time when the transportation network is more important than ever to the nation's prosperity. Modern business methods, such as just-in-time inventory, rely increasingly on an effective transportation system.

Figure I-1 provides insights into one aspect of America's current transportation policy failure. It displays vehicle miles traveled (VMT) and available lane miles from 1980 to 2007, both indexed so that 1980 equals 100. Roughly speaking, VMT reflects the (largely unpriced) demand for the service provided by America's road, highway, and tunnel network, while lane miles reflect supply. VMT has almost doubled over the period, while the increase in available lane miles is negligible. Clearly, under the current approach, the supply of lane miles has fallen far short of demand for transportation services. This reflects a failure both to manage demand adequately and to increase the supply of transportation facilities.

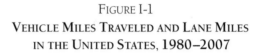

FIGURE I-1
VEHICLE MILES TRAVELED AND LANE MILES
IN THE UNITED STATES, 1980–2007

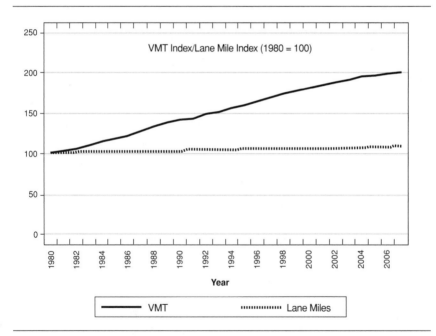

SOURCES: For lane miles, see Department of Transportation, Research and Innovative Technology Administration, Bureau of Transportation Statistics, "Table 1-6: Estimated U.S. Roadway Lane-Miles by Functional System," http://www.bts.gov/publications/national_transportation_statistics/html/table_01_06.html (accessed May 26, 2010). For vehicle miles traveled, see U.S. Census Bureau, *The 2010 Statistical Abstract of the United States,* "Table 1065—Motor Vehicle Distance Traveled by Type of Vehicle," http://www.census.gov/compendia/statab/2010/tables/10s1065.xls (accessed May 26, 2010).

Why does an innovative, industrialized nation like the United States face these problems in such a critical sector? The reasons go well beyond a simple "unwillingness to fund" transportation infrastructure. America's transportation problems reflect an underlying failure in our basic approach and can be addressed only through a fundamental shift in policy. Fortunately, there is a new approach that will result in a customer-oriented, efficient, and adequately financed surface transportation system. It has the potential to reduce congestion, generate sufficient funds to upgrade America's surface transportation system and maintain it over the long term, and reduce the politicization of transportation investments. This new approach has three main components:

- Pricing of transportation services, or charging motorists based on their use of transportation facilities

- Congestion or value pricing, which utilizes appropriate charges for customers who choose to use a facility when it is most valuable—that is, during periods of peak demand

- Reliance on private investment to help fund surface transportation infrastructure

Road pricing and congestion pricing both interact with private investment in important ways, as I discuss below. And although any of these three elements would improve transportation system performance, I focus here primarily on the third, which includes investment in highways, bridges, and tunnels. The analysis also applies to other transportation infrastructure, such as intermodal connectors, ports, and airports. The emphasis of this book is on *why* transportation PPPs should be done rather than on *how* to do them. The question of how best to implement transportation PPPs could easily fill another volume.

The distinction between greenfield and brownfield PPPs is important to understand for the purposes of this book. In a greenfield PPP, a private entity (perhaps a consortium of firms) is engaged through a contractual agreement to design, build, finance, and then operate a new transportation facility. The new facility may be tolled or untolled. In a brownfield PPP, the agreement allows a private firm to manage, operate, and renovate an existing (usually tolled) facility. This distinction is important because greenfield and brownfield PPPs raise different policy issues. When properly executed, both types generate substantial benefits for customers, investors, and citizen-owners.

The book proceeds as follows. In chapter 1, I discuss the above three key elements in detail. This includes an analysis of the serious problems associated with ongoing fuel-tax funding of transportation infrastructure, as well as the importance of charging for road use according to the costs imposed by the motorist on the facilities and on other motorists. In chapter 2, I define PPPs more precisely and list some examples of standard PPP approaches. I then survey several PPP concession agreements concluded in the United States.

In chapter 3, I compare firm governance (or "public control") in PPPs with that in alternative organizational approaches, such as a public toll authority model. I show how firm governance is improved by the PPP approach.

In chapter 4, I present the rationale for PPPs in more detail. I discuss several commonly recognized benefits of PPPs, such as accelerated project delivery and lower operational costs. I also highlight some less-appreciated advantages of PPPs, which include the social gains from greater competition in the design, construction, operation, and maintenance of transportation assets; sharper incentives to innovate; improved safety; and enhanced public control over transportation assets, among others. Although accelerated project delivery applies to greenfield projects only, the other benefits articulated in this chapter also apply to brownfield PPPs.

In chapter 5, I explain the benefits of PPPs to investors, as well as the social advantages of transferring risk to those investors. I consider the new opportunities that private infrastructure investment offers for institutional investors, such as pension funds, insurance companies, and university endowments. I also discuss several policies to help promote PPP use and close the chapter by discussing how PPPs help to rationalize transportation investment.

In chapter 6, I focus on the benefits of brownfield leases. I show how they unlock latent value for the citizens who own these facilities. I also address several criticisms of brownfields, such as concerns about misuse of concession proceeds and intergenerational equity issues. I close by discussing some recent policies designed to promote further private participation in U.S. transportation.

In chapter 7, I summarize the voluminous empirical evidence on private participation in industry generally, which includes assessment of many industries and countries, as well as evidence for the beneficial effects of private participation in transportation specifically. I also provide a brief survey of the use of transportation PPPs abroad.

Although their benefits are numerous, PPP agreements should not be concluded in haste. They must be carefully designed and executed to realize the greatest public benefit and avoid future problems. In chapter 8, I suggest a few of the issues that potential public sponsors may wish to consider prior to entering into a PPP. These include the management of the PPP process, the development of expertise in public-private interactions, the use of innovative auction approaches, the enforcement of contracts, and the regulation of market power, among others. Following chapter 8 is a summary and conclusion.

America's transportation problems are formidable, but they are solvable. A dramatic change in perspective is called for, however, on the part of those who utilize the system as well as those who own it. Commuters, vacationers, truckers, and delivery companies should cease thinking of themselves as mere "users" of the transportation system, and instead insist on being treated as the customers who pay for it. Citizens should cease thinking of themselves as disconnected and alienated from the transportation network (other than in their capacity as motorists), and begin thinking of themselves as the system owners they truly are. Citizen-owners must demand that their facilities be well maintained and, since they ultimately bear the risk associated with those facilities, that they receive a reasonable return on their investment. Citizens need to become active, engaged owners of U.S. transportation facilities. Finally, policymakers need to think about the best framework to bring the suppliers and the demanders of capital together to make the system more accountable—and valuable—to both its motorist-customers and its citizen-owners.

The United States is a first-world nation with a second-rate surface transportation system. It deserves a system that does not sap the inherent energy and productivity of American workers but instead facilitates and amplifies those qualities. When policies are implemented that allow private participation to reach its full potential, it will achieve just that.

1

Three Critical Transportation
Policy Reforms

America's current approach to transportation policy has failed the country. It has resulted in worsening congestion, chronic underinvestment, deteriorating infrastructure, and politicized and increasingly uncertain financing. The motorists who use America's roads, highways, bridges, and tunnels pay dearly for that policy failure every day through diminished quality of life. These problems cannot be corrected by simply raising fuel taxes to underwrite further government spending under the current approach. Rather, America's severe transportation problems call for a new vision for its transportation system.

The purpose of this chapter is to discuss the three policy changes that will most dramatically improve the U.S. transportation system. They are a shift toward direct road pricing rather than the financing of roads based on fuel taxes, allowing road prices to vary with demand (or value) to allocate scarce road capacity, and encouraging a major infusion of private capital through PPPs to fund the renovation of existing facilities and the construction of new ones.

The Problem with Fuel Taxes

America's surface transportation system is funded in a different way at each level of government. At the federal level, roads, bridges, highways, and transit are largely funded through the Highway Trust Fund. Revenues from federal motor-fuel taxes, vehicle fees, and a few other sources flow into the Highway Trust Fund, which has three components: the highway account, the mass-transit account, and the much smaller leaking underground storage-tank account. The federal government redistributes the majority of those funds back to the states in a bill (passed roughly every six years) that reauthorizes transportation spending using a complex formula. The remainder is allocated through earmarks.

TABLE 1-1

FEDERAL, STATE, AND LOCAL REVENUES USED FOR HIGHWAYS
(BY COLLECTING AGENCIES) FROM VARIOUS SOURCES, 2005
(AS PERCENTAGE OF TOTAL)

Source	Federal		State Agencies		Local		Total	
	Amount	%	Amount	%	Amount	%	Amount	%
Motor-fuel and vehicle taxes	$31,179	20	$49,176	32	$2,234	1	$82,589	53
Tolls	—	—	$6,356	4	$1,398	1	$7,754	5
Property taxes and assessments	—	—	—	—	$7,811	5	$7,811	5
General fund appropriations	$1,488	1	$3,384	2	$17,233	11	$22,105	14
Other taxes and fees	$388	0	$4,291	3	$4,620	3	$9,299	6
Investment income and other receipts	$15	0	$2,897	2	$5,199	3	$8,111	5
Bond issue proceeds	—	—	$11,622	8	$5,400	3	$17,022	11
Grand Total Receipts	**$33,070**	**21**	**$77,725**	**51**	**$43,895**	**28**	**$154,690**	**100**

SOURCE: National Surface Transportation Policy and Revenue Study Commission, *Transportation for Tomorrow: Report of the National Surface Transportation Policy and Revenue Study Commission*, 2007, vol. 2, ch. 5, exhibit 5-2, http://transportationfortomorrow.com/final_report/pdf/volume_2_chapter_5.pdf (accessed November 12, 2009).
NOTE: A dash indicates that this source does not exist for this level of government. Percentages may not sum to totals in columns due to rounding.

As shown in table 1-1, fuel taxes account for over 90 percent of the revenues into the federal Highway Trust Fund and for over 50 percent of highway spending at all levels of government.[1] Other revenues come from tolls, motor-vehicle taxes, general funds, and bonds. At the state and local levels, bond issues are an important source of revenues. At the local level, the largest source of revenues is general fund appropriations. Tolls currently constitute a small portion of the total revenue used to fund highways, accounting for 4.5 percent in 2004, although that proportion is increasing rapidly. Between 2000 and 2004, for example, revenues from tolls in the United States grew by 21 percent, while revenues from fuel taxes and vehicle taxes grew by only 2.5 percent and 0.1 percent, respectively.[2]

Although Oregon levied highway-dedicated fuel taxes in 1919 (and all states had done so by the 1930s), construction of the Interstate Highway System greatly increased America's dependence on dedicated fuel taxes. President Dwight D. Eisenhower, one of the prime movers behind the Interstate Highway System, preferred tolls, but the primitive toll-collection technology of the time would have required motorists to stop and pay a toll-booth operator.[3] Frequent stops would have defeated the purpose of a high-speed, limited-access highway. When construction began in earnest on a system of interstate highways in the mid-1950s, fuel taxes were consistent with a fee-for-road-use approach. Since most passenger cars realized similar gas mileages, fuel and road use were roughly correlated, so a fuel tax was the next best thing to a toll.

Importantly, both the federal gasoline tax (currently 18.4 cents per gallon) and the federal diesel tax (currently 24.4 cents per gallon) are levied, as indicated, on a cents-per-gallon basis and do not change with inflation.[4] Federal fuel taxes have not been increased since 1993, and the purchasing power of revenue from those taxes has decayed by about one-third since that time.

Many recent failures of the U.S. surface transportation system stem from continued reliance on fuel taxes. At least three policy problems are associated with an ongoing reliance on a funding approach based on fuel taxes, as described below.

Fuel-Tax Funding Conflicts with Other National Policy Goals. First, reliance on fuel taxes to fund transportation is problematic because it conflicts directly with other important national policy goals. A desire for greater fuel economy, lower emissions, and energy independence has led the United States to adopt policies aimed at reducing fossil-fuel use for transportation.

The main policy tool to increase vehicle fuel efficiency has been the Corporate Average Fuel Economy (CAFE) standard, which was adopted in the wake of the 1973 oil embargo. CAFE standards are requirements for the average fuel economy (miles per gallon) of a manufacturer's current fleet of cars or light trucks. These standards have become more stringent over time. In December 2007, President George W. Bush signed into law a bill that requires auto companies to achieve a fuel-economy standard of thirty-five miles per gallon by 2020, with substantial improvements by 2015. In May 2009, President Barack Obama further increased the stringency of CAFE standards, to an average of thirty-nine miles per gallon for cars and thirty miles per gallon for trucks by 2016.[5]

Improved efficiency through stricter CAFE standards will reduce revenue realized from a cents-per-gallon fuel tax. A subsidy to encourage a move to hybrid vehicles will have a similar effect, as will a shift to alternative power sources, such as electricity, ethanol, and hydrogen. Policymakers' desire for greater fuel economy appears to be intensifying, so the outlook for sustained, reliable funding of the transportation system through fossil-fuel taxes is bleak at best. Indeed, there is evidence that the increasing fuel efficiency of the vehicle fleet is already straining state transportation budgets. As the *Wall Street Journal* reports, "Cars and trucks are getting more fuel efficient, and that's good news for drivers. But it's a headache for state highway officials, who depend on gasoline taxes to build and maintain roads."[6]

Fuel-Tax Funding Is Inherently Unstable. The second problem with relying on fuel taxes for transportation funding is that, aside from policies that actively discourage fossil-fuel use, fuel-tax revenues are inherently unstable due to basic market forces. Crude-oil prices are set in a global market and determined by the basic forces of supply and demand. Supply-side factors include environmental constraints, potential cartelization, security threats (such as terrorism directed at oil-producing and refining facilities), and instability in the Middle East, among many others. Demand factors include the availability of substitutes and the expansion of large economies, such as those of China and India, whose rapid development can absorb substantial amounts of petroleum products.

Because suppliers cannot respond quickly to large increases in demand, fossil-fuel prices are prone to sharp upward spikes, which generate a wide variety of both short- and long-run responses from motorists. They may make any of a vast number of adjustments, including choosing more fuel-efficient vehicles (including electric cars, hybrids, motorcycles, and scooters), changing driving habits (such as driving more slowly and combining shopping trips), using public transit, carpooling, walking, biking, changing home or work locations, or telecommuting.

These responses cause instability in miles driven and, thus, in fuel use. In March 2008, for example, vehicle miles traveled on U.S. public roads fell by 11 billion from March 2007—a 4.3 percent decline, and the sharpest drop in recorded history. Fluctuations in VMT highlight the problems associated with a fuel-tax approach to funding infrastructure. The 2008 VMT reductions were likely related to the 2007–2008 increases in retail gasoline prices: U.S. gasoline prices rose dramatically from roughly $2.25 per gallon on February 12, 2007, to a high of roughly $4.10 per gallon on July 12, 2008, and then declined sharply.[7]

Inflation is another important cause of revenue instability. Inflation generally, and inflation in highway construction and repair costs in particular, erodes the purchasing power of revenue from fuel taxes over time. To make matters worse, highway-related costs have been rising faster than overall inflation. For example, burgeoning construction activity in large developing economies has bid up the cost of materials. Between 2003 and 2006, the Federal Highway Administration Bid Price Index increased 48 percent, while the Consumer Price Index (CPI) rose by only 10 percent.[8] Combined with the long lead times required to complete major highway construction projects, these factors add to the instability of the purchasing power flowing from fuel taxes.

Moreover, because a large fraction of oil supplies is imported, monetary policy affecting exchange rates also has an impact on fuel prices. If, for example, monetary policy is accommodative (that is, the money supply is increasing to stimulate growth) and generates low interest rates, the dollar is likely to fall, driving up the dollar price of imported crude oil and reducing fuel consumption.

These forces are already affecting balances in the federal Highway Trust Fund.[9] The federal government, like many states, has reverted to using general revenues for transportation funding. The highway account would have experienced a large shortfall had Congress not allocated a direct taxpayer infusion of $8 billion.[10] Consequently, the Government Accountability Office added the nation's federal highway programs to its list of high-risk programs, which is intended to identify weaknesses in programs that involve substantial resources and provide critical public services. Based on these projections, Congress gave the fund a direct taxpayer infusion of $8 billion in September 2008 and another $7 billion in July 2009.[11] Partly as a result of those infusions, transportation experts have questioned the long-term viability of the trust fund concept itself.[12]

Fuel-Tax Funding Breaks the Link between Consumers and Producers. A third important yet underappreciated problem with fuel-tax funding is based on simple economics: tax funding breaks the link—normally provided by prices—between the value motorist-consumers place on the transportation services provided by roads, bridges, and tunnels, and the way those transportation dollars are directed to particular facilities. The consequences are dire.

There are two broad approaches to directing investment into or out of any activity: through markets or through a political process.[13] One advantage of allocating investment via markets is that prices provide a direct link between the value customers place on a good or service and the movement of dollars into or out of the production of that good or service. Markets and prices are the mechanisms that direct investment in the production of automobiles, bread, books, and the vast majority of goods and services produced in the United States. Systems that have generally not relied on markets and prices to direct investment into the production of basic goods, such as the Soviet Union or the Chinese economy under communist principles, have failed. Systems relying on markets and prices to allocate resources have thrived.

In a market setting, customers let suppliers know how much they value a service by their willingness to pay for it. Suppliers stand to receive higher returns from investing in projects and activities where customer values, and thus prices, are higher. The converse is true for lower prices—that is, lower customer values. Profit-maximizing suppliers respond to the prices customers are willing to pay by adjusting how much they invest in the service and the type of investment they provide. Market-based direction of investment is, therefore, inherently customer-focused.

The main alternative to markets for allocating investment is a political process in which centralized planning of one sort or another directs investment. Since customers don't pay directly for a good or service, there is no objective measure of the value they place on it. Without a price to provide information on customer value, suppliers of transportation services must use information only weakly related (or unrelated) to willingness to pay in determining where to add road capacity. Although planners may try to infer customer values through various methods, it is easier for special interests with political clout to influence the process of allocating investment dollars. Investment is more likely to be steered into their preferred projects, regardless of whether those projects represent the most economically valuable use of the funds.

Political preference thus comes to supplant motorist-customers' objective values, and spending becomes politicized and misdirected. The ultimate transportation customers—the commuters, truckers, and vacationers who use the roads—become, at best, secondary to the process. Even the prevailing transportation lexicon reflects this: customers are typically not referred to as such by the providers of transportation services, but are instead referred to as road "users." The term "user" strongly implies a non-market paradigm, different from what Americans have come to expect from the providers of almost all other services. In transportation under a fuel-tax funding approach, customers' preferences are simply less important. The focus is not on providing a valuable service, but on building projects consistent with planners' targets.

Conversely, from the perspective of the motorist-customer, reliance on fuel taxes has the effect of hiding the true cost of maintaining and expanding these assets. Because they are imbedded in the price of fuel, fuel taxes reduce the salience of the tax payment to consumers.[14] This furthers the absurd perception that highways, bridges, and tunnels are "free" rather than, in fact, enormously expensive assets to build and maintain. The perception of free transportation infrastructure further encourages its overuse. Road pricing has the important benefit of informing road customers of the true cost of constructing and maintaining such assets.

In light of all these problems, a consensus is emerging within the transportation policy community that the fuel-tax approach to infrastructure financing has outlived its usefulness and that change is needed. For example, in 2009 the National Surface Transportation Infrastructure Financing Commission concluded that,

> looking forward, a variety of factors are converging to challenge the pre-eminence of MFTs [motor-fuel taxes] as the primary source of surface transportation funding. Due to a combination of travel growth, system deterioration, increasing construction costs, and lack of indexing, fuel tax revenues are becoming increasingly inadequate to meet investment needs. This inadequacy will likely be exacerbated as improved fuel efficiency and the development of alternative fuel vehicles reduce fuel consumption. Moreover, the public's willingness to pay for the required investments through an increase in motor fuel taxes appears to be weak and may be declining.[15]

Similarly, John L. Mica, a Republican representative from Florida and ranking member of the House Committee on Transportation and Infrastructure, stated flatly that "the gas tax, as the mechanism for funding transportation improvements, is obsolete."[16] I consider the benefits of an alternative approach below.

A Better Strategy: Fee for Road Use

Linking transportation infrastructure financing to a tax on fossil fuels is a flawed long-term strategy presenting myriad problems. A better strategy could be based on the same direct "fee-for-service" or "fee-for-use" principle that applies to the use of any utility. Just as customers are charged per kilowatt hour of electricity consumed, per gallon of water used, per minute of phone use, or per therm of natural gas, road customers can be charged per mile for the use of a particular facility.[17] Technologies now available ensure that road pricing can be done anywhere with no slowdown in traffic whatsoever, alleviating the concerns of an earlier era that toll booths would cause excessive delays. Electronic tolling also allows the classification of vehicles according to the cost they are likely to impose on the facility they are using.

At least two approaches to collecting tolls electronically have been used: centralized collection and fuel-pump collection. Under centralized collection, data on a vehicle's road use are sent from an onboard transponder to a center that periodically bills the customer. Typically, an overhead gantry reads the onboard electronic device. This is coupled with license-plate recognition (and billing) for those without a device. A cash-only option is provided for those who prefer anonymity. Centralized collection appears to be most appropriate for single, relatively high-volume facilities.[18] Many different facilities across the country are now using such an approach, however, and it is possible to drive across numerous states using a transponder issued by a single firm.

An important innovation, sticker tags, has further lowered the cost of centralized toll collection. Sticker tags, which are very small (about 2.5 inches by 1 inch) and very inexpensive (less than $5), are placed on vehicle windshields, allowing the vehicles to use numerous toll facilities. They have been deployed widely in Mexico and Brazil and are considered successful there. In the United States, sticker tags have been issued by the company TransCore in Florida, Texas, and Georgia. The low cost of using them is certain to increase the number of motorists who rely on electronic tolling. Even with the adoption of sticker tags, however, nontrivial costs are associated with centralized toll collection, including the installation and maintenance costs of sticker-reading equipment, as well as such "back office" costs as salaries for customer service and license plate–reading personnel.

Another, less frequently used, method is to charge motorists a mileage fee at the point of fuel sale. The most comprehensive test of this type of road pricing in the United States to date, completed in November 2007, was conducted by the Oregon Department of Transportation.[19] In it, each participating vehicle contained a device that identified the vehicle's movement within various predetermined zones. Mileage-data input and fee collection occurred at the fuel pump. The station attendant presented the motorist with a bill including both the mileage fee and the purchase price of the fuel, net of state fuel tax.[20] The test indicated that a mileage fee could be implemented gradually while retaining a fuel tax, as vehicles equipped with reading devices replaced nonequipped vehicles in the fleet.

Improvements in electronic tolling continue apace. A recent innovation that could be rapidly deployed was developed by engineers at the University of Minnesota. A plug-in device that measures and logs vehicle miles traveled, it utilizes a data-link connector that is already installed in all North American vehicles manufactured after 1996, as well as existing cell phone networks.[21] No new wireless or roadside infrastructure is necessary to utilize the device, which could be in widespread use in several years. Yet another new technology, Skymeter, is thought to be significantly better than standard global positioning systems (GPS) in providing accurate vehicle locations in dense urban environments.[22]

Regardless of the method chosen, establishing a system of road pricing is an important step toward meaningful surface transportation policy reform. When used in conjunction with private investor participation, it reestablishes the link between the desires of motorist-customers and the suppliers who provide the facilities that fulfill those desires. Providers of transport services have an incentive to be attentive to customers' needs and desires, and to keep them on the facility rather than off.

From the citizen-owners' perspective, road pricing converts a road, bridge, or tunnel that would otherwise be a drain on the government's budget into an asset that produces income. When an asset produces income, owners have a stronger incentive to rehabilitate, expand, and maintain the facility.

Americans appear to recognize the advantages of road pricing over fuel taxes for funding transportation investment. When confronted with a choice between road pricing and higher fuel taxes, they overwhelmingly prefer pricing. A survey conducted by the Colorado Department of Transportation found that citizens favored tolling over fuel taxes by a margin of 66 percent to 16 percent. Similarly, a national opinion poll conducted by the American Automobile Association found that 52 percent of respondents favored tolls as a way to fund expanded highway investment, while only 21 percent favored increased fuel taxes. A survey of the Washington, D.C., area by the *Washington Post* found a margin of 60 percent to 30 percent in favor of tolls over taxes. A 2007 survey in King County in Washington State found that, by a margin of 77 percent to 17 percent, respondents preferred financing the reconstruction of a major bridge with electronic tolling instead of gas taxes.[23] Other surveys have found a similar preference for road pricing over fuel taxes, implying that the public may accept pricing when it understands the choice between these two alternatives.

Meanwhile, evidence suggests that fuel taxes are becoming less popular. This may be related to their severe regressivity, meaning that they fall disproportionately on lower-income groups. A 2007 study by the comptroller of the State of Texas, for example, found that the gas tax was by far the most regressive of all the taxes that the state levies, including sales taxes, franchise taxes, natural gas taxes, and property taxes.[24] The declining popularity of fuel taxes is also suggested by the Tax Foundation, which states in its 2007 *Annual Survey of U.S. Attitudes on Tax and Wealth* that

> at the state and local level the most unfair tax was the gasoline tax, which received an unfairness ranking of 3.8 on a scale of 1 to 5. State gas taxes range widely throughout the nation from a low of 7.5 cents per gallon in Georgia to a high of 38.65 cents per gallon in New York. This finding came as a surprise, as previous surveys have generally found local property taxes to be the most disliked state and local tax.[25]

Changes in fuel efficiency across vehicles have also rendered fuel taxes less fair. They were viewed as fair when they were increased to fund the construction of the Interstate Highway System because, as mentioned earlier, the amount paid in tax at that time was roughly correlated with road use. Passenger vehicles then were comparable in size and weight and thus realized similar gas mileage. Vehicles today are quite different in size and weight, with concomitantly differing gas mileages. The relationship between road use and taxes paid has thus weakened over time, which may contribute to the increasing unpopularity of fuel taxes. Used in isolation, however, road pricing presents a major challenge: how to ensure that the monies paid by motorists are actually used to maintain and upgrade the relevant transport facility, or in support of transportation at all. That is, if not accompanied by other policy changes, road pricing potentially creates the same "diversion of revenue" problem that has plagued fuel-tax funding.[26]

Congestion Pricing: Paying According to Cost

Although a move toward using direct road pricing rather than fuel taxes to finance roads is an important step in improving transportation policy, its effect on traffic congestion will be limited unless the price or toll charged varies with the costs that one motorist imposes on all the others by choosing to use a particular facility at a particular time.[27] Similar to a pipe with water flowing through it, or a wire along which electrons move, a road, bridge, highway, or tunnel has a physical capacity limit: a lane can only transport a certain number of vehicles per hour. When many motorists try to use a facility at the same time, the facility becomes congested, like a clogged pipe. Traffic flow collapses, and the bridge, highway, or tunnel is unable to handle nearly as many vehicles as its physical capacity allows (that is, when traffic is flowing freely). Traffic inches along, bumper to bumper, and traveling even a short distance is time consuming. Most drivers in the United States are all too familiar with this phenomenon.

Economically speaking, when drivers decide to use their vehicles, they incur a number of costs. These include the cost of fuel, depreciation of their vehicles, time spent driving, and wear and tear on transportation facilities, as well as the crowding out of other motorists who want to use the facilities at the same time. The drivers will bear many of those costs directly, and will therefore take them into account in their decisions about when, how often, and how far to drive. They will, for example, bear fuel costs, vehicle depreciation, and time costs. Since they will not, however, bear directly the costs associated with facility wear and tear or the crowding out of other motorists who also want to drive at that time, they will not take them into account in their driving choices. Their decisions will thus not be aligned with the true overall cost of using particular facilities at particular times.

Facility wear-and-tear costs can easily be addressed through a fee for road use. The second component, however, is more complex, since motorist crowding has "nonlinear" effects on travel time. That is, as a facility gets close to its physical limits, even a small increase in the number of vehicles leads to a large drop in the speed of all vehicles. If one additional motorist tries to use the road at those peak times, he or she imposes a large cost on all other motorists through slower travel times. The motorist who decides to use a highway at 3:00 a.m. imposes no crowding or congestion costs on other motorists, since there is usually plenty of road space, while the one who instead uses the highway at 8:00 a.m., when many other motorists also want to use it, imposes substantial congestion costs. Under the current approach, the individual motorist does not consider those large social crowding costs.

The second aspect of road pricing is thus a variable charge, or congestion price, to reflect the costs of social crowding. The phenomenon noted above suggests the effectiveness of such charges. If even a small number of motorists can, through congestion prices, be encouraged to drive at other times, to use alternative modes of travel, to carpool, to telecommute, or to adjust in any number of other ways, then traffic flow will rise disproportionately to the number of motorists who choose *not* to use the facility at that time. Sometimes reducing the number of drivers by as little as 5 percent at peak times will enable traffic to flow smoothly, allowing the same facility to handle many more vehicles.[28]

Variable road prices therefore have the effect of allocating scarce road space at peak times to those who most value it. They will choose to use it at those times and pay the associated higher fee. Under the current approach, available transportation capacity is allocated by queuing, or waiting in line. While queuing may be acceptable for seating at a restaurant, it is a very wasteful method of apportioning something as important as space on a transportation facility. Queuing ignores the cost that one motorist imposes on others in trying to use a facility at peak times, as well as the differing values motorists place on the road's use at particular times.

Because congestion prices keep traffic moving smoothly, travel times also become more predictable. This is critical to parents, for example, who need to pick their children up (or drop them off) from school or day care at specific times. It also reduces the time wasted in planning for possible congestion, or in leaving a time cushion to allow for travel uncertainty. Furthermore, congestion prices help ensure that facilities are used more evenly throughout the day.

Congestion pricing is not a novel concept. As noted, similar variable charges have been successfully utilized in other industries—for pricing, for example, airfares, cell phone rates, electricity rates, room rates at hotels and resorts, and fares on Amtrak and some local transit systems. Congestion pricing has also been used successfully on a number of U.S. roads. It is currently used in Minneapolis on the I-394 MNPass Express Lanes, which are dynamically priced in real time. It is used on the I-15 FasTrak Lanes in San Diego, where prices are updated every six minutes, and on the I-25 express lanes in Denver. It is also used on the SR-91 Express Lanes in Orange County, California, where the price varies between $1.15 and $9.25 per trip and is posted prior to entry so motorists can choose between priced and nonpriced lanes. Priced lanes have been popular because they save substantial amounts of time.[29] The Oregon pilot program mentioned earlier indicated that variable pricing could be incorporated into an overall pricing approach.[30]

Many international examples of the use of congestion pricing are also available. In 1975, Singapore became the first city to implement it successfully for urban traffic. Under this approach, called the Area Licensing Scheme, cars were charged an additional fee to enter the central business district between 7:30 a.m. and 9:30 a.m. This form of congestion pricing, known as cordon or central area pricing, was strikingly successful, resulting in a 73 percent decrease in the use of private cars, a doubling of bus usage, and a 30 percent increase in carpooling.[31] In 1995, congestion pricing was extended to three of Singapore's major freeways. On one freeway, average speed during the peak hour increased from 31 to 67 kilometers per hour. Other examples of cities using congestion pricing include Bergen, London, Oslo, Stockholm, and Trondheim.[32]

In addition to the demand-side benefit of helping to manage traffic flow, variable pricing creates another, supply-side, benefit: it provides information on how much motorists value the use of particular facilities and thus reveals the most valuable investments. Prices reveal value, and the amount of the congestion price required to smooth traffic flows is a reflection of how much value motorists place on a facility. Relatively high prices suggest that motorists place a high value on using that facility during peak times. The social returns to expanding the road, bridge, or tunnel will thus also be high, and investment should be directed there.

By providing an objective indication of where expansion of the system should or should not take place, congestion prices also help depoliticize transportation investment, making it more efficient.[33] As the quotations below suggest, a consensus has emerged that tolling (and, importantly, PPPs) can provide objective information on where investment should take place and reduce political influences in transportation spending. As transportation expert Robert Poole, for example, writes,

> The phrase "bridge to nowhere" several years ago became the symbol of out-of-control earmarking of highway and transit projects by members of Congress. One of my ongoing themes is that an excellent way to bypass this kind of wasteful spending is to use the "filter" of toll financing (and better yet, long-term toll concessions). The point is to substitute economic criteria, like return on investment, for the political criteria often used in selecting projects. In order to develop a toll road or toll bridge, the proponents need to demonstrate to those providing the funds that the project is so useful that its customers will pay enough, over time, to recover its cost of construction and operation.[34]

Poole goes on to discuss four new toll-bridge projects in which this principle is illustrated. Another prominent analyst is former Congressional Budget Office director Douglas Holtz-Eakin, who echoed the points made above:

> Introducing congestion pricing on a crowded highway—that is, charging tolls that are higher during peak times of the day and lower during off-peak ones—has two economic effects. First, it dampens demand for the highway during the most congested periods by inducing some motorists to alter their travel plans. Some drivers will be able to modify their schedules so they use the road at less busy times. Others will find alternative routes or switch to public transit. Second, continued demand in the face of appropriate congestion pricing serves as a signal for additional investment in road capacity.[35]

The 2007 *Economic Report of the President* similarly states,

> In addition to improved allocation of road space, charging a fee also provides urban planners with useful information about

when and where to invest in the expansion of existing road capacity. Expansion should be focused on roads where drivers demonstrate a willingness to pay that is higher than the cost of construction.[36]

Alan Day, a professor of economics at the London School of Economics, states explicitly that road pricing should be a guide to investment:

> It is quite indefensible to argue as many do that road pricing should simply be used to ration existing road space. Road pricing should be used both as an allocative device and as a measure of whether or not to add to or subtract from the existing road space. It can and should be used as an investment criterion....
>
> If road users are prepared to pay a price for the use of roads that is greater than the costs of providing additional road space (including all costs, externalities etc.) then the additional road space should be built, and as in any other economic activity, the charge for the use of the new facility should be sufficient to finance its cost.[37]

Finally, the supply-side benefits of road pricing have been emphasized by Nobel laureates in economics for decades. Writing in the early 1950s, Milton Friedman and Daniel J. Boorstin noted that

> at first glance, it seems hardly possible that this apparently trivial problem of how to charge people for the highway services they use is a key to the whole problem of how to plan and pay for better highways; yet it is just that. This fact cannot be too strongly emphasized. It is a key not only for a system that would involve operation of roads by private enterprise but equally for the present system of public operation. Should a particular road be built? How should it be built? How should it be financed? Should an existing road be maintained, improved, or allowed to deteriorate? If we could charge directly for the service of the road, we could answer those questions—whether under private or public ownership—in the same way that we now decide how

many automobiles should be manufactured, what kind of automobiles should be manufactured, how their production should
be financed, whether a particular model should be discontinued, and so on.[38]

In short, road pricing and congestion pricing would yield important
benefits on both the demand and supply sides of the transportation sector.
It is not sufficient, however, simply to provide suppliers with signals and
information about how much motorist-customers value the expansion of
particular facilities. Suppliers must also have both the capital and the
incentives to respond aggressively to this information. That requires
greater participation by private firms—the third critical step in transportation policy reform, which I will now begin to explore in depth.

Private Investment in Transportation Infrastructure

PPPs, road pricing, and investment choices interact in important ways. For
example, as noted above, an important social benefit of facility pricing is
that it allows motorists to recognize the costs they are imposing, both to the
facility itself and to other motorists in the form of congestion, and to take
them into account in their behavior. Once they face those costs, motorists
can then choose their own best way of adjusting to them.

Systematic differences in the way government and private firms are
likely to price have long been recognized. In particular, the prices charged
by government firms will tend to be less reflective of the costs of serving
different types of customers than those charged by private firms.[39] Prices
charged by government firms will thus be less effective in informing
transportation customers of the costs they impose on the facility and
others, and consequently less effective in giving motorists an incentive to
adjust appropriately to those costs. This is not controversial. The Government Accountability Office emphasized the advantage of private participation in this respect, and noted how it leads to enhanced infrastructure
condition and performance, in its analysis of PPPs:

Highway public-private partnerships potentially provide benefits by better pricing infrastructure to reflect the true costs of operating and maintaining the facility and thus realizing public benefits of improved condition and performance of public infrastructure. In addition, through the use of tolling, highway public-private partnerships can use tolling techniques designed to have drivers readily understand the full cost of decisions to use the road system during times of peak demand and potentially reduce the demand for roads during peak hours.[40]

Private partners are also more likely to accept the risks associated with more innovative pricing approaches, such as time-of-day and vehicle-based pricing. This is distinct from the adoption of pricing technology itself, such as electronic toll collection.

The participation of private investors in transportation infrastructure funding has many additional advantages. As I discuss below, it brings added capital to bear and so allows projects to be built and renovations to occur that would otherwise be severely delayed or postponed indefinitely. It also transfers to investors the risks that would otherwise be borne by taxpayers. The details of the PPP contractual agreement are critical, however, to achieving these salutary outcomes. The agreement specifies the roles, risks, and rewards to both the public and private partners. A properly designed PPP contract will ensure that the transportation facility is operated in the public interest while at the same time protecting the private party's investment, so private capital will continue to flow into such projects in the future. In the following chapter, I discuss some common types of contracts and provide some examples of transportation PPPs in the United States.

2

Basics of Public-Private Partnerships

Investor participation in the financing of U.S. toll roads has a long history. According to Daniel B. Klein and John Majewski, between 2,500 and 3,200 companies successfully financed, built, and operated private toll roads during the nineteenth century.[1] The combined mileage of those roads at any one time was between 30,000 and 52,000 miles. The 946 incorporations of turnpikes between the years 1800 and 1830 comprised about 27 percent of the total number of incorporations during that period. Similarly, Robert E. Wright and Brian P. Murphy have found that at least 7,000 private corporations in the United States operated roads, bridges, canals, ferries, and railroads by 1860, comprising a large portion of U.S. gross domestic product.[2] Moreover, private timber companies have long constructed roads and bridges on public lands to take advantage of logging rights. Private investors have also long held the municipal bonds traditionally used to finance many transportation projects.[3]

Extensive private investment in financing, constructing, and operating U.S. transportation infrastructure is not new to the United States. However, some terminology and concepts surrounding private participation have changed over time. I begin my discussion of PPPs by providing some basic information about these agreements as they have evolved in recent years.

PPP Terminology

Public-private partnerships range from concessions of highway rest stops to arrangements in which private partners help to design, finance, build, operate, own, and/or manage major transportation facilities. Definitions of PPPs are invariably broad. According to the Government Accountability

Office, highway PPPs refer to "highway-related projects in which the public sector enters into a contract, lease, or concession agreement with a private sector firm or firms, and where the private sector provides transportation services such as designing, constructing, operating, and maintaining the facility, usually for an extended period of time."[4] Similarly, the U.S. Federal Highway Administration website on PPPs states that "Public-Private Partnerships (PPPs) are contractual agreements formed between a public agency and private sector entity that allow for greater private sector participation in the delivery and financing of transportation projects."[5] Because that is where some of the largest benefits lie, the focus of this book is on PPPs that facilitate increased private financing of transportation projects, and where private investors assume some risks inherent in the construction and operation of transportation projects.

Terminology pertaining to transportation PPPs, particularly brownfields, has created unnecessary confusion. A variety of terms have been used to describe those PPP contracts with varying degrees of accuracy, including toll concessions, leases, franchises, asset sales, and privatizations. "Asset sale" and "privatization" do not accurately describe U.S. PPPs, since those terms imply a change in facility title and a possible loss of control by the public partner. No ownership change has taken place with respect to any U.S. transportation PPP to date; facilities instead always remain publicly owned.[6] A toll concession, for example, is simply a long-term lease. If a landlord owns a structure with an apartment upstairs and a storefront downstairs and leases out her storefront, this does not "privatize" or "sell" the structure. It remains owned by the landlord.

Moreover, as I show below, PPPs enhance rather than diminish true public control over transportation facilities. For example, PPP contracts allow performance standards to be clearly articulated, unlike arrangements with public-sector entities. PPPs also allow for meaningful penalties if standards are not met and for rewards if they are exceeded—that is, PPPs allow performance standards (sometimes called key performance indicators, or KPIs) to be enforced. They also ameliorate inherent agency problems between a facility's owners—the citizens of the relevant jurisdiction—and its managers.

The terms "lease," "franchise," and "toll concession" better describe the contractual and ownership dimensions of brownfield PPP arrangements.

"Lease," "toll concession," and "PPP" are sometimes used interchangeably, although PPPs can and do involve facilities that are untolled.

PPPs allow private investors to channel capital into critical transportation facilities, including light-rail systems, ports, and intermodal connectors, as well as highways, bridges, and tunnels. They can be used to help finance construction of new facilities or to refurbish, expand, and better manage existing ones. In the United States and abroad, as noted earlier, PPPs have also been used to finance nontransportation projects, including wastewater treatment plants, desalination plants, hospitals, schools, prisons, and many others. As these broad definitions suggest, there is no single type of PPP. In transportation, however, there are some useful contractual categories. Contract types illustrate the breadth and versatility of the PPP approach.

Types of PPP Contracts

PPP contractual agreements are notable for their diversity and flexibility. No two PPP contracts are exactly alike. They can be adapted to suit the needs and circumstances of the public sponsor while attracting and protecting private investment. Although they can be adjusted along a host of dimensions, they can be more simply and usefully classified by the degree of public versus private responsibility they assign. Roughly speaking, moving from the least amount of private responsibility to the greatest, some common contractual categories include the following seven:[7]

- *Design-bid-build (DBB)* was the traditional contractual approach used to construct many public works in the United States in the twentieth century. Under a DBB contract, the public sector engages engineers and architects to design a facility to meet certain specifications. It then accepts bids from precertified construction firms to build the facility. Notably, the design and construction firms in a DBB contract are separately responsible for each of those project stages. The government is responsible for financing the project and assumes all risks associated with its ownership and operation. The facility remains under government management for its entire design life. Private financing and risk assumption are minimal in a DBB contract.

- A *design-build (DB)* contract is a straightforward extension of a DBB contract. Under a DB approach, a single private partner designs and constructs a facility, in contrast to the separation of those responsibilities in a DBB contract. A DB contract has the advantage of allowing one firm to use its information, knowledge, and skill to coordinate a facility's design with its construction. Like DBB contracts, DB contracts usually do not involve private financing, but private parties do assume additional risk through the design and construction process.

- With the *design-build-operate-maintain (DBOM)* approach, parties can benefit from an integration of processes beyond that offered by the DB contract. Under a DBOM arrangement, the private partner is responsible for the design, construction, operation, and maintenance of a facility for a specific time period. Operation and maintenance functions are therefore added to the responsibilities a private partner carries in a DB contract. Payment after project completion is conditional on meeting certain performance standards, such as physical condition, traffic congestion, ride quality, and capacity. A DBOM contract allows the private partner to utilize its detailed knowledge of a particular facility's design and construction to develop a maintenance and operating plan specific to that facility. By assigning responsibility to the private partner for project quality and performance throughout its entire lifecycle, this approach also gives the contract team an incentive to provide the best possible plan and project. If, for example, heavy vehicles are going to use a highway, then a private firm that maintains as well as builds the facility has an incentive to use more durable pavement.[8] The government typically retains ownership and is responsible for financing the project under a DBOM contract.

- *Long-term lease (LTL)* agreements allow the competitively chosen private partner to lease an existing toll facility for an extended time period through a bidding process. Brownfield PPPs are LTL contracts. The contract details the responsibilities of the private partner regarding maintenance, operation, improvement, and expansion of the facility in return for the right to the facility's toll revenue. The private partner typically pays an upfront concession fee, although other approaches, such as revenue sharing or annual lease payments, are possible. Ownership again remains with the government, but private investors usually assume risks—such as revenue risk from changes in traffic flow, as well as risks associated with changes in operation, maintenance, and renovation costs. In the United States, the Indiana Toll Road and the Chicago Skyway concession agreements (see below) are examples of long-term leases.

- A *design-build-finance-operate (DBFO)* contract is an extension of the DBOM approach in that the private partner assumes at least some added responsibility for financing the project and for the risks associated with that financing—that is, the private partner becomes responsible for the design, construction, financing, operation, maintenance, improvement, and expansion of a new facility. The partner is granted the right to actual toll revenue (or shadow toll payments; see below) for a specified time period in exchange for fulfilling those responsibilities. Although DBFO contracts vary according to the degree of private financing involved, part of the financing is usually accomplished through debt that leverages streams of toll revenue. A DBFO contract may be awarded for the upgrading or expansion of an existing facility if the necessary renovations are significant. In many cases, operational responsibility reverts to the government after a period of time. This appears to be a popular approach internationally.

- Under a *build-operate-transfer/build-transfer-operate (BOT/BTO)* contracting approach, the private partner designs, constructs, finances, and operates the facility, as under a DBFO contract. The BOT and BTO approaches differ when legal title to the facility is transferred. In the BOT approach, transfer takes place at the end of a predetermined franchise period. In the BTO approach, transfer typically takes place at the end of the construction period. This and related approaches have been used globally. In Australia, for example, facilities have been built and operated under a build-own-operate-transfer (BOOT) approach.

- A *build-own-operate* (BOO) contract engages the competitively chosen private partner in a broad range of responsibilities, including the design, financing, construction, ownership, maintenance, and operation of a transportation facility. Because the private partner actually owns the facility, it assumes all risks associated with the facility's ownership and operation. Although there is no obligation for the public sector to purchase the facility or take title, the terms of the concession may be adjusted, or the government may purchase the facility.

These contractual examples, while far from exhaustive, illustrate the ways in which PPPs allow private partners to assist public-sector sponsors in a range of transportation activities. In all of the arrangements described above in which motorists actually pay tolls, the private partner receives the toll revenue. This is referred to as a "real toll" arrangement.

Alternative approaches in which private partners do not receive toll revenue include shadow tolls and availability payments. Shadow tolls are payments made by the public sector to a private road operator based, at least in part, on the number of vehicles using the road. Payments can incorporate the type of vehicle and the distance traveled.[9] Tolls are "shadow" (as opposed to "real") in the sense that motorists do not pay them directly. Multiple sources of public funds can instead be used to support shadow tolling. Depending on their structure, such tolls allow public and private partners to share traffic (or demand) risk. They also allow PPPs to be used on untolled roads, which is an important advantage.

Availability payments are similar to shadow tolls in that the private partner does not receive toll revenue directly. Unlike shadow tolls, the public partner makes a payment that is not based on traffic volume.[10] Rather, payment is based on other dimensions of service quality, including such factors as safety, congestion, minimum performance criteria, and lane availability. Although the government assumes demand risk under this approach, other important risks can be transferred to private partners. Availability payments also cap the public sector's obligations.

Shadow tolls are used in the United Kingdom, Spain, Portugal, and several countries in Eastern Europe. Real tolls, shadow tolls, and availability payments can be used in various combinations on the same facility over time. For example, a facility can begin with shadow tolls only, then phase in a shadow/real toll combination as traffic volume increases, and phase out shadow tolls altogether when traffic volume becomes sufficient to make the facility self-supporting.

The first application of availability payments to a transportation project in the United States will be on the I-595 corridor roadway improvements in South Florida.[11] Completion is expected in spring 2014. The core of the project is the reconstruction and widening of I-595 near Fort Lauderdale. According to the U.S. Federal Highway Administration, the project will be operated as an availability-payment PPP with several important innovations, including reversible, congestion-priced lanes.[12] Customers will, however, pay a real toll set by the government, with all revenue retained by the government. The payment to the private partner is based on a detailed set of performance criteria, with specified downward adjustments if standards are not met.

Shadow tolls and availability payments are not without their disadvantages. For one, any approach that does not actually charge motorists for using the facility does not generate the critical incentives created by real tolls to conserve on facility use.[13] Additionally, because private sponsors will not be serving motorists directly (the government is their sole customer), they are unlikely to develop the strong customer-service orientation engendered by a real toll arrangement. In the I-595 case, the government will receive toll revenue. As with fuel-tax funding or VMT charges, however, revenues may be diverted away from the facility or away from transportation altogether, thus weakening the user-pays principle.

Transportation PPPs in the United States

The following brief descriptions of completed transportation PPPs in the United States illustrate various contractual agreements and project types, and the courses they have taken. They will be referred to periodically throughout the chapters that follow.

California 91 Express Lanes. The 91 Express Lanes combine a ten-mile, high-occupancy toll road with a full tollway lying completely within the median of State Route 91 (the Riverside Freeway) in California. Opened in 1995, the express lanes are separated from the regular SR 91 lanes by three-foot yellow plastic lane markers. There are no tollbooths in the lanes, and all tolls are collected electronically using FasTrak transponders. To help manage congestion, the toll lanes use time-of-day pricing (as opposed to real-time, variable tolling).

The project was developed through a partnership between the California Department of Transportation (Caltrans) and the California Private Transportation Company (CPTC). In April 2002, the Orange County Transportation Authority (OCTA) agreed to purchase the lanes for $207.5 million, and it took possession in January 2003. The lanes are managed and operated by Cofiroute USA, which is one of the primary investors in the project.[14]

The 91 Express Lanes are notable for several firsts, all of which are relevant to the central argument of this book. In explaining their decision to assign the 1996 Excellence in Highway Design award to the 91 Express Lanes, the U.S. Department of Transportation's Federal Highway Administration stated that "Ninety-One Express Lanes is the world's first automated toll road; the first implementation of congestion pricing on a U.S. toll facility; and the first toll road to be privately financed in the U.S. in more than 50 years."[15]

The 91 Express Lanes were controversial because of a noncompete clause contained in the PPP agreement. Noncompete clauses are designed to prevent loss of revenue due to competing nearby free roads and have been used to protect bondholders on both publicly and privately financed roads. The clause precluded construction by the state of competing facilities along thirty miles of the Riverside Freeway. CPTC filed a lawsuit against

Caltrans when the state widened parts of the freeway.[16] Although the lawsuit was dismissed after OCTA purchased the facility, the controversy caused changes in the nature of many noncompete agreements. The controversy and its outcome provide an example of how the United States learns from experience with PPPs over time and how experience can improve the quality of public-private contracting.

Chicago Skyway. The Chicago Skyway concession is an example of a long-term leasing, or brownfield, PPP contract. The Skyway is a 7.8-mile toll road that is part of the I-90 interstate highway. It connects the Dan Ryan Expressway (which carries both I-90 and I-94 route numbers) in Chicago to the Indiana Toll Road (I-90). A 3.5-mile section of the Skyway is elevated, allowing it to cross the Calumet River. The Skyway carried about 50,000 vehicles per day in 2005.[17]

In March 2004, the City of Chicago issued a request for qualifications from bidders interested in leasing the Skyway for a ninety-nine-year term. The city received ten responses, and five bidders were asked to submit detailed proposals. The high bid of $1.83 billion came from a partnership of Cintra Concesiones de Intrastructures de Transporte S.A. (Cintra) of Madrid, Spain, and the Macquarie Infrastructure Group of Sydney, Australia, which cooperated to create the Skyway Concession Company LLC (SCC). The city awarded the contract to SCC in the first modern long-term lease of an existing U.S. toll road.[18]

The SCC has the right to all concession and toll revenues from the Chicago Skyway. Annual toll increases are capped at the greatest of 2 percent, the rise in the Consumer Price Index, or the increase in U.S. gross domestic product per capita. The $1.83 billion upfront payment was equivalent to an impressive 70 percent of the city's annual budget.[19] Although I emphasize in later chapters that the advantages of PPPs do not stem from the way in which public sponsors decide to use concession proceeds, it is nevertheless instructive to examine how they were used here. Some uses of the $1.83 billion payment include: $825 million to pay off both outstanding Skyway and city debt; $500 million to creating a reserve fund that will produce about $25 million annually for the city; $325 million was invested in an annuity; and $100 million went to a variety of projects, such as homeless shelters, facilities for senior citizens, and libraries.[20]

Moody's Investor Service upgraded Chicago's bond rating as a result of its improved fiscal position to the highest level in twenty-five years.[21]

Importantly, by revealing the true market value of the facility, this brownfield PPP allowed the citizens of Chicago to know and consider the rate of return they were earning as owners of the Skyway under city management. Given the income and expenses of the Skyway and the $1.83 billion market value of the concession as revealed through the bidding process, citizen-owners were receiving an abysmal 0.4 percent return on their investment.[22] Taxpayers were therefore much better off paying down debt, which carried an interest rate of about 5 percent—over twelve times what they were earning prior to the lease.[23] And the private partner improved the operation of the road by, for example, quickly adopting electronic tolling.

As this summary suggests, most of the proceeds from the concession fee were used for nontransportation purposes. The agreement has been criticized for that reason, with some justification, since it raises concerns similar to those associated with fuel-tax funding or a VMT charge, namely, how to ensure that toll revenue paid by motorists is used for transportation or, better yet, on the facility in question.[24] There is an important conceptual distinction (discussed later in more detail) between brownfield concession fees and either fuel-tax or VMT revenue, however. Brownfield concession fees are properly thought of as compensation to facility citizen-owners for previous value creation, just as an initial public offering of stock or any other sale of a firm is compensation to investors for value already created. The value is embedded in the facility, and the lease agreement extracts some of it. In contrast, fuel taxes and VMT fees are typically thought of as ways to charge for current facility use. One might therefore argue that citizen-owners have more liberty to spend lump-sum concession proceeds as they see fit than they do with a stream of motorist payments for current use. Public acceptance of a brownfield approach seems to be greater, however, when there are assurances that proceeds will be used for transportation purposes, perhaps reflecting concerns about how wisely fee proceeds would be used otherwise.

Denver Northwest Parkway. The Northwest Parkway is a nine-mile toll road outside of Denver, Colorado, forming a portion of the (incomplete)

Denver beltway. Construction on the parkway began in June 2001, and it opened to traffic on November 24, 2003. The parkway struggled financially its first few years. In November 2007, the Northwest Parkway Public Highway Authority entered into a concession and lease agreement for its operation and maintenance with the Northwest Parkway LLC, a joint venture between the Portuguese firm Brisa Auto-Estradas S.A. (known simply as Brisa) and the Brazilian firm Companhia de Concessões Rodoviárias (CCR). This arrangement was unusual, and laudable, in that a toll authority itself leased responsibility for its operations.

Brisa and CCR paid $603 million for the concession rights. The parkway authority used the proceeds to pay off remaining construction-financing debts and provide funding for a 2.3-mile extension of the toll road connecting to State Highway 28 in Broomfield, and also put funds into an escrow account to provide incentive payments for local jurisdictions.[25] These payments will be used to mitigate local opposition to the completion of the missing portion of the overall Denver beltway.

Dulles Greenway. The Dulles Greenway is a fourteen-mile, limited-access highway outside of Washington, D.C. It extends from the state-owned Dulles Toll Road—which connects the Washington, D.C. Capital Beltway going from Dulles Airport to Leesburg, Virginia—and it opened to traffic in September 1995.

The Dulles Greenway offers an interesting case study of the versatility of private investment arrangements. Its structure does not fit into standard modern PPP categories and may instead be best described as a recent example of a facility built under a nineteenth-century toll road charter. Indeed, its website notes that "the Dulles Greenway is one of the first highways of its kind in the United States, and is the first private road in Virginia since 1816."[26]

The Greenway was built under the Virginia Highway Act of 1988. Interestingly, the 1988 act did not grant the investors—the Toll Road Investors Partnership II (TRIP II)—the power of eminent domain. Rather, the assemblage of private lands required to build the Greenway was purchased at market price.[27] Also unusual is the Greenway's regulation by the Virginia State Corporation Commission, which limits its rate of return to 18 percent, similar to utility-style regulation. Unlike with standard utility regulation, however, the Greenway receives no legally enforced monopoly through an exclusive territory. It continues to pay real estate taxes on property purchased to build the road, thus generating tax revenue that would not be forthcoming under a traditional public-ownership approach.[28]

The Greenway was financed at a cost of $350 million by TRIP II, with $40 million in equity and $310 million in privately placed taxable debt. Ten institutional investors held most of the debt. Under the original agreement, operational responsibilities were to revert to Virginia after 42.5 years. The Greenway faced financial challenges in its early years, however. TRIP II restructured its debt in 1999, and the Virginia State Corporation Commission extended the concession length by twenty years, to 2056.[29] Tolls were increased in September 2004, and different peak and discounted off-peak rates were allowed. TRIP II sought regulatory approval for more variably priced tolls in July 2006, consistent with a congestion-pricing approach.

TRIP II was purchased by the Macquarie Infrastructure Group in August 2005 for $617.5 million and is now a fully owned subsidiary of Macquarie. The road is, however, operated by Autostrade International, which is a subsidiary of the world's largest toll road operator, Italian-based Autostrade S.p.A.[30]

Indiana Toll Road. The Indiana Toll Road is the second example of a brownfield long-term leasing arrangement. In operation since 1956, the 157-mile road runs along the northernmost border of Indiana. The toll road is an important transportation facility in a broader sense, linking large cities on the eastern seaboard with those on the Great Lakes.[31]

The Indiana Department of Transportation operated the toll road for many years. In 2005, the State of Indiana issued a request for proposals for a seventy-five-year lease and received four. The winning offer was for $3.8 billion from the Indiana Toll Road Concession Company (ITRCC), which again was a joint venture between Cintra and Macquarie.[32] The concession agreement placed limits on toll increases and on the concessionaire's return on investment. The state was committed to using the proceeds to fund a ten-year plan known as Major Moves, which would support about two hundred transportation projects around the state. As a result, Indiana became the only U.S. state with a fully funded transportation plan for the years 2006 to 2015. Major Moves will ultimately result in a quadrupling of highway spending in Indiana, from $213 million in 2006 to $874 million in 2015.[33] As in Chicago, where Moody's Investor Service upgraded the city's bond rating as a result of the Skyway concession's fiscal benefits, the Indiana brownfield concession led Standard & Poor's to upgrade the state's debt rating to AAA, its best rating ever. The improved debt rating will save the state millions of dollars in interest payments over time. The lease is widely viewed as successful.

I-495/Washington, D.C., Beltway HOT Lanes. The Washington, D.C., region generally and the Northern Virginia area in particular are among the fastest-growing areas in the country. The amount of traffic using the Capital Beltway overall has tripled since it was last expanded in 1997, and congestion costs the local economy almost $5.5 billion a year.[34] Unsurprisingly, the Northern Virginia portion of the Capital Beltway is one of the most congested traffic routes in the eastern United States.

Assistance is coming in the form of fourteen miles of high-occupancy toll (HOT) lanes to be added to the Northern Virginia portion of the beltway, the first major expansion in over thirty years. HOT lanes are tolled lanes that operate alongside existing untolled highway lanes. The goal is to provide motorists with faster, more reliable alternative lanes. In this case, two new HOT lanes will run in each direction. Carpool vehicles (defined here as carrying three or more occupants), buses, motorcycles, and, of course, emergency vehicles will all have free HOT lane access. Vehicles with fewer than three occupants can choose to have access to the lanes by paying a toll. Importantly, dynamic tolling (that is, congestion pricing) will be used on the HOT lanes to ensure traffic remains free flowing at all times. Tolling will be fully electronic, using transponder technology.[35] According to the Virginia Department of Transportation,

> The I-495 Virginia HOT Lanes Project will deliver the most significant enhancement to the beltway since its opening in 1964. The project includes two new lanes in each direction from the Springfield Interchange to just north of the Dulles Toll Road and the replacement of more than $260 million in aging infrastructure. This includes replacing more than 50 bridges, overpasses, and major interchanges.[36]

The Capital Beltway HOT lanes will be financed, built, and operated through a fixed-price, design-build PPP. In June 2002, the Virginia Department of Transportation (VDOT) received an unsolicited proposal from Fluor Daniel to design, build, and finance the Capital Beltway HOT lanes. The proposal was received through Virginia's Public-Private Partnership Act of 1995, which allows private parties to enter into transportation PPP agreements with the state and provides for unsolicited proposals. VDOT invited competing proposals, but received none.[37] In October 2004, VDOT and Fluor became aware of the need for a skilled facility operator on the project team and accepted Transurban Limited, a new participant on Fluor's project team, as an additional project partner in the negotiations.[38] A comprehensive development agreement was concluded in December 2007, under which a partnership of Fluor Enterprises and Transurban would construct and operate the lanes, while VDOT would own and oversee them.[39] The lanes will be completed in 2012 with the first tolling beginning in 2013. The total concession life is eighty-five years, with five years of construction and eighty years of operation. The total project cost, estimated at $1.9 billion, is being financed using a mixture of sources, including private equity, private activity bonds, TIFIA loan financing (described later in the book), and a $409 million grant from the state. This is one of the largest financings of HOT lanes in the United States and the first time private activity bonds have been used to help fund HOT lanes. Importantly, the project's large cost and state fiscal constraints would likely have prevented it from moving forward without private investment.[40]

Texas State Highway 130. Texas State Highway 130 is also known as Pickle Parkway (after former congressman J. J. "Jake" Pickle), or SH 130. This tollway will, when completed, be eighty-nine miles long and run in a corridor south and east of Austin.[41] SH 130 was constructed to help address the large increase in truck traffic between the United States and Mexico associated with the passage of the North American Free Trade Agreement, which came into effect on January 1, 1994. It serves as an alternate route to I-35, which it parallels.[42]

Lone Star Infrastructure, a partnership of civil engineering firms and large highway-construction firms, was awarded a contract to build one major section of SH 130 in 2002. The first segment was opened to the public in November 2006. In June 2008, Cintra-Zachry reached an agreement with the State of Texas to build segments five and six. Cintra-Zachry will have the right to collect tolls on those segments for fifty years in return for their investment of $1.3 billion. The agreement caps toll rates, which will rise at the rate of inflation. Cintra-Zachry and the state will share toll revenue. Title to the road remains with the state. The concessionaire is responsible for designing, constructing, operating, maintaining, and, importantly, financing the facility. As an indication of the capital-raising advantage of PPPs, a tax-exempt, debt-only approach using toll revenue bonds would have raised about $600 million, while a PPP was able to raise the entire $1.3 billion using a combination of debt and equity.[43] As with the Capital Beltway HOT Lanes, it is unlikely that the SH 130 project would have been built without private financing.[44]

To summarize, PPPs are described in many ways, but they are in essence simply contractual arrangements between a public sponsor and private partners to design, construct, finance, operate, and/or maintain a transportation facility. Notwithstanding an array of permutations, such contracts are a straightforward extension of the standard design-build contracts that public sponsors have utilized for decades. Recent PPP arrangements incorporate greater private financing and, consequently, added risk assumption by the private sector. Although the advantages of greater private participation in financing, renovating, maintaining, and managing transportation facilities flow from somewhat obvious extensions of current policy, they are, as will be stressed in chapters 4 and 5, substantial.

PPPs have already been used successfully in the United States in numerous ways and on a variety of projects. They are relied upon to renovate and expand existing facilities and to construct new ones. They have been used to allow the citizen-owners of a facility to realize its value, while at the same time improving its management and operation. One underappreciated aspect of PPPs, however, is their effect on firm governance. I explore those effects in the next chapter, before moving on to review the benefits of PPPs more generally.

3

Compared to What?
Why Private Investor Participation
Is Needed

Critical to understanding the importance of public-private partnerships is to consider the arrangements upon which they seek to improve. Debate often focuses on simplistic questions along the lines of, "Are PPPs good or bad?" Such phrasing overlooks the most basic of policy questions: compared to what? PPPs cannot be analyzed in a vacuum, but instead must be compared to prevailing alternative approaches to delivering transportation facilities and related services.

There is broad appreciation in the policy debate that more private participation through PPPs can inject additional, desperately needed capital into America's transportation system. Analysts also often mention the risk-shifting benefits that flow from private investor participation. The larger implications of PPPs for a firm's incentives generally, and for firm governance in particular, are less well appreciated.

In this chapter, I explore the effects of private participation on firm governance. To do so requires comparing governance under a PPP—that is, provision of transportation facilities and services by a private firm—with that under the most appropriate government counterpart, the state-owned enterprise (SOE). An SOE is typically defined as a government-owned firm that, similar to many PPPs, has its own revenue source.[1] In the transportation sector, a toll authority meets that definition.

Governance under Bureaucratic Administration

Governance is a broad term, popularized over the past decade, that refers to a common problem faced by all firms (except sole proprietorships), whether publicly or privately owned: how do the firm's owners (also called its "principals") ensure that the firm's managers (the "agents" appointed by the principals) behave in the owners' interest rather than in their own? This basic conflict, known as the principal-agent problem, occurs in any organization in which owners appoint others to manage the firm on their behalf. Governance refers to the way the agency problem is addressed in any organization and includes the host of arrangements and processes that have evolved over time to deal with it. Governance requires owners to spend time and money choosing the right managers, providing them with appropriate incentives (through compensation arrangements and/or the threat of removal, among other mechanisms), maintaining transparent operations, and watching over, or "monitoring," their performance.[2]

To appreciate the impact of PPPs on governance, one must compare them with other organizations providing the same services. Currently, most transportation facilities are managed either by a state department of transportation or, more commonly for toll facilities, by a state or municipal toll authority.

Vital to effective firm governance are specific, clear-cut goals on which managers can focus. Since a toll authority SOE has no well-defined, active group of owners, its goals remain fuzzy, open to debate, and susceptible to external influence. Should the firm work to depress tolls as much as possible, even if the facility loses money? Should it strive to increase the number and job security of its employees? Should it focus on simply breaking even over time? Should it maximize traffic throughput, regardless of costs? The lack of a concentrated, effective group of firm owners implies that such questions have no clear answers. Exhortations for SOE managers simply to operate "in the public interest" offer little guidance.

The result is an absence of managerial accountability—that is, a more severe agency problem. When performance is deficient in one area, managers can simply claim they were focused on a different goal, with the choice of goal influenced by the group or groups that are the most politically effective at any given time—whether unions, environmentalists, consumer groups, or, less frequently, taxpayers. SOE agency problems should not be blamed on the choice of managers, however, since they occur even with dedicated people in place. According to the World Bank,

> Bureaucrats typically perform poorly in business, not because they are incompetent (they aren't), but because they face contradictory goals and perverse incentives that can distract and discourage even very able and dedicated public servants. The problem is not the people but the system, not bureaucrats per se but the situations they find themselves in as bureaucrats in business.[3]

The lack of a well-defined, active group of owners comparable to that of a private firm also means that no one bears directly the consequences—through tangible changes in its members' wealth—of managerial decisions. Although the citizens of a state or municipality nominally own transportation assets, they are a highly diffuse group, so the effect of improved management on any one of them is negligible. The amount a taxpayer stands to gain from being an "activist owner" of a transportation facility is trivial and difficult to capture, so his or her incentive to monitor managers actively and improve performance is accordingly weak. The result has been striking governance failures in transportation SOEs, some examples of which I will examine after exploring in more detail the impact of private participation on firm governance. This requires careful consideration of the nature of private firm ownership.

Private Investment Improves Governance

To appreciate the effects of government ownership on firm performance, we must first consider the concept of a residual claim. A residual claim is simply a property right to a firm's net cash flows. The person or group holding that property right is called a residual claimant. Firms are identified by the nature of their residual claims. If one person is the residual claimant, then the firm is a sole proprietorship. If a group of partners are the residual claimants, then the firm is a partnership. If shareholders are the residual claimants, it is a corporation, and so on. In a state-owned enterprise, the residual claimants are the citizens of the relevant jurisdiction. If the SOE is a municipal toll authority, the citizens of the municipality are the residual claimants.

A hallmark of the residual claims of the large modern corporation is that they are freely tradable in a market—the stock market—at fairly low cost. The social value of that tradability is difficult to overestimate. One key effect is that the act of trading residual claims in a market generates a price for those claims, one that is widely published and continuously updated. The stock price thus continuously reveals the value that investors place on the firm. This has an important effect on firm governance, since stock prices provide objective information about managerial performance. A decline in a firm's stock price, perhaps relative to the industry's average, may be a sign of poor managerial performance, and conversely.

Another key benefit of tradable residual claims is that both individual and institutional shareholders—such as pension funds, mutual funds, university endowments, and insurance companies—can accumulate large share blocks.[4] Because of their substantial wealth stake, large shareholders have especially strong incentives to monitor managers actively and help overcome the principal-agent problem.

Those governance benefits of tradability cannot be realized under SOE ownership. SOE residual claims are not tradable, so no market for them exists.[5] This means they are not priced, so no objective indicator of firm value, and thus of managerial performance, exists. It is thus impossible to easily measure managerial performance and tie it to compensation. Moreover, nontradability means that citizen-owners cannot accumulate the concentrated ownership in the firm that would give them the incentive to carefully monitor managerial performance. Therefore, no one citizen-owner has the incentive to be an active owner of transportation facility assets.

An additional hindrance to firm governance created by nontradability is heterogeneity of citizen-owner interests. Citizens are a highly diverse group and typically do not share the same objectives for a particular transportation investment—that is, they have not self-selected into holding equity in a transportation facility, as would private investors. Their objectives for the facilities they nominally own will thus be vague and wavering. Partly because of this lack of focus caused by poorly defined ownership, more concentrated, better-organized groups may gain control of SOEs and exploit them for their own gain.

Aside from the absence of strong incentives and adequate information, citizen-owners have few tools at their disposal to act on poor managerial performance. Under bureaucratic administration, managers' compensation is typically determined by civil service pay scales, and could not be related to firm performance even if transparent performance measures existed.[6] Additionally, it is very difficult for citizen-owners to remove government firm managers for poor performance. It is difficult, for example, even for a state's governor to remove a senior toll-authority manager.

In fact, the only mechanism typically available to citizen-owners to control a toll authority—via the governor's board (or "commission") appointments—is highly indirect. Voters elect the governor, which causes an agency problem between citizens and the governor. The governor then appoints the facility's board, which causes a second agency problem between the governor and the board. This injects at least one more layer of agency between citizen-owners and their appointed managers than in a typical corporation, where shareholders elect the board directly. Faced with few external control devices, such as proxy votes, incentive-pay packages, managerial removal, or hostile takeovers, SOE managers have little incentive to operate transportation facilities efficiently.[7]

One might argue that citizens could vote for new political representation in an attempt to monitor and control transportation facility managers, but that decision is likely to be conflated with an array of other issues affecting citizens' voting choices. Moreover, the likelihood that any particular voter will affect the outcome of an election is tiny, so voters will not invest the time and effort necessary to become informed about transportation issues and how their votes might matter.[8] For all of these reasons, citizens are likely to be weak, inactive, and ineffective owners of transportation facilities. The fact that few citizens even think of themselves as transportation facility owners is testimony to that fact.

The cumulative effect of these limits on the incentives and tools of citizen-owners to control government transportation firms is to weaken constraints on managerial behavior. The managers of a government firm are more likely to deviate from citizen-owners' interests and to exercise their own discretion. Subject to legal constraints on the firm, they may do this in a variety of ways, such as basing appointments on political patronage rather than managerial ability, expanding managerial power by increasing the organization's size and scope, and focusing managerial decisions on placating well-organized pressure groups, among others.

In addition to providing capital and absorbing risks that would otherwise be assumed by citizen-owners, private investment brings powerful—and beneficial—incentives to bear in an industry in dire need of them. In particular, it brings incentives to maximize profits. Profit maximization in turn gives the firm incentives both to increase its revenues and to lower its costs. Those paired goals cause the firm to adopt a customer orientation, to utilize the latest technology, and to conduct its operations efficiently. Such focused objectives create what are sometimes referred to as "hard" incentives, and they are essential to firm governance.[9]

In short, PPPs strengthen incentives by introducing a concentrated group of owners who stand to gain directly from better firm performance and who are harmed directly by poor performance. Although private owners may be heterogeneous in other attributes, in their capacity as investors their interests are uniform: they are focused on improving firm performance.[10]

The strong incentives introduced by a concentrated group of investors who bear directly the wealth consequences of managerial decisions has salutary effects on governance. If a facility is maintained, well run, and expanded appropriately, then the firm will perform better, and private investors stand to receive greater returns.[11] If a facility is operated poorly, so that costs rise unnecessarily and service quality deteriorates, customers will use alternatives, profits will fall, and investors will receive lower returns. As a concentrated group that bears the impact of good or bad managerial decisions, private investors have strong, direct, and immediate incentives to ensure that facilities are operated and maintained as efficiently as possible. Although this is true generally, it is also recognized by transportation-sector analysts specifically. "In particular," Chris Meads and Bryce Wilkinson write in reference to road management,

> private ownership would be likely to provide more effective monitoring and commercial incentives for the firm's management than public ownership. Private investors would be placing their own wealth at risk by investing in the firm, and would therefore have more incentive to monitor and take an active interest in the commercial performance of the firm and its management.[12]

To provide specifics, suppose a new technology, such as electronic toll collection, lowers operating costs. Because they stand to gain directly from its application, private investors have powerful incentives to ensure that the technology is adequately funded and that managers adopt it as quickly as possible. Without well-defined, effective owners who stand to gain from—and are willing to take the risk of—its implementation, new, cost-saving technology is adopted only slowly, if ever.[13]

Moreover, private investors have additional tools at their disposal to improve firm governance that are unavailable under any type of bureaucratic administration. As noted, tradable residual claims generate a stock price, which provides an objective, updated measure of managerial performance. Additionally, in sharp contrast to SOEs, private investors have direct control over executive-pay plans and can structure them in creative ways. They can use salary, restricted stock, stock options, and bonuses tied to stock performance, among other mechanisms, to ensure that overall compensation varies with firm performance, thus aligning managers' incentives with those of firm owners. Such flexible compensation arrangements are of enormous assistance in ameliorating the agency problem in transportation. The National Surface Transportation Infrastructure Financing Commission, for example, noted that "a private operator whose compensation is performance-based has a strong incentive to strive for maximum operational efficiencies and to grow revenues by providing strong customer service."[14]

Clearly, then, private participation in the transportation sector in the form of public-private partnerships offers major advantages in terms of effective governance of the firms delivering transportation services. Below I describe some specific experiences of firm governance—or the absence of it—under the prevailing SOE approach that will help address the question, "Compared to what?" as we explore transportation PPPs in the chapters ahead.

The Governance Experience in Public Toll Authorities

A comparison between a PPP and a toll authority is appropriate because both usually have managerial control over a transportation facility that generates its own toll revenue. From a governance perspective, control of toll revenue is an important distinction between facility operation by a toll authority and that by a state or municipal transportation department. State legislatures and governors control transportation department budgets, while toll authorities have an independent revenue source through tolls and other fees, which effectively makes them state-owned enterprises. Budgetary control over transportation departments and their subunits provides a monitoring tool unavailable to citizens for improving the governance of toll authorities.

The combination of multiple objectives, lack of stock price information, weak managerial incentives, inability to concentrate ownership, and the very limited governance tools available to citizen-owners has generated a history of poor governance of toll authorities. In Massachusetts, for example, events in 2002 illustrate the degree to which senior toll authority managers are insulated from citizen-owner control. In May of that year, Governor Jane Swift tried to remove two Massachusetts Turnpike board members for voting to delay a toll increase. The Massachusetts high court ruled that the governor—the directly elected representative of the turnpike's citizen-owners—acted beyond her powers in firing the two board members, and reinstated them. The court ruled that only "malfeasance, misfeasance, or willful neglect of duty" were sufficient grounds for dismissal.[15]

This very high standard for removal of government managers that follows from the toll authority's legal structure results in managers becoming entrenched. In contrast, the shareholders of a publicly traded firm can remove the board of directors via proxy vote at any time without cause.[16] The responsiveness of managers to shareholders of publicly traded corporations (as well as firm value) would plummet if such a strict legal standard were applied to managerial removal by their boards.

In another example, in 2006 a three-ton section of the ceiling in the Massachusetts Turnpike I-90 tunnel connector—part of Boston's "Big Dig" project—collapsed and killed a thirty-eight-year-old motorist named Milena del Valle. Citing this event after a series of other serious managerial failures, Governor Mitt Romney sought the removal of Matthew Amorello as chairman and chief executive officer of the Massachusetts Turnpike Authority. One might expect that a state governor could immediately remove an appointed manager and his team for such a profound failure, but, again, court approval was necessary. Although Amorello resigned before a court decision was rendered, this episode further illustrated the extreme autonomy—and almost complete lack of accountability to a facility's citizen-owners—enjoyed by government-firm managers as compared to their private-sector counterparts.

Unsurprisingly, this lack of accountability also manifested itself through abuses of governance processes under Amorello. One commentator described the situation prior to the chairman's resignation:

> Amorello increasingly treated the Turnpike as his private fiefdom. At a poorly attended board meeting [in] late June he rammed through bylaws giving him full personal discretion over calling board meetings, and full control to set the meeting agenda. As chairman he could rule any non-agenda items out of order. This rendered him totally unaccountable, and the board powerless. As chairman he could refuse to allow a vote of no confidence in his chairmanship, for example. It wasn't on the agenda. He hadn't put it there, so it couldn't be discussed.[17]

Shareholders would never tolerate such poor governance in a publicly traded corporation in an era when sound corporate governance is widely recognized as a critical goal. Private managers attempting such abuse would be removed by the board, by existing shareholders through proxy, or by outside takeover. It would be a mistake, however, to conclude that such abuse is due to the individual personalities involved and that it could be addressed through the appointment of more selfless, independent, civic-minded persons. Such a complete breakdown in governance is, instead, due to the firm's organizational structure. In the absence of active, private owners who may exercise effective governance tools, any organization that controls an independent revenue source will eventually be exploited for private gain.

Such problems are not, of course, limited to Massachusetts. Another state in which toll authority governance has been questioned is Texas, where toll authorities have been referred to as a "power unto themselves."[18] And in yet another example of a toll authority's autonomy, in 2006, the Pennsylvania Turnpike Commission advised the governor of Pennsylvania—

again the directly elected representative of the owners of that same toll authority—that

> the Commission is an independent instrumentality of the Commonwealth, which is directed by a five-member Board. Because of its autonomous nature, the Governor's control over matters governed by the Commission is "limited to those powers expressly conferred to him by statute or constitution."[19]

Given the focus today on accountability and sound corporate governance, one might be concerned about the board of a large, publicly traded company reminding the shareholders of its "autonomy."

It is likely that such lack of accountability will manifest itself in the use of Pennsylvania Turnpike resources for personal and parochial gain. That is, indeed, the case. Political patronage on the Pennsylvania Turnpike has been detailed in two books by William Keisling, *When the Levee Breaks: The Patronage Crisis at the Pennsylvania Turnpike, the General Assembly and the State Supreme Court* and *Helping Hands: Illegal Political Patronage in Pennsylvania and at the Pennsylvania Turnpike*. A complete discussion of the turnpike's governance problems is beyond the scope of this book, but several points are noteworthy. Keisling implicitly recognizes that citizens are ineffective owners and notes that political patronage on the Pennsylvania Turnpike includes not only jobs, but various types of contracts as well:

> The two political parties for all practical purposes own the Pennsylvania Turnpike Commission…. To help facilitate the awarding of jobs each party since 1985 has employed a patronage boss, officially known as assistant executive directors for the western (currently a Republican) and eastern (currently Democrat) regions. Their job has been to help the party bosses…dole out jobs to the party faithful. The booty is not just jobs. Billions of dollars in all sorts of contracts are awarded.[20]

Keisling also notes specifically the deleterious effect of an independent revenue source when an organization lacks true investors. "Over the years the turnpike became a figurative dumping ground of state patronage," he writes. "Endless revenues from the tolls early on made it a cashbox for state politicians."[21]

Toll authority governance problems are, unfortunately, not limited to recent times. Indeed, the above examples of diversion of toll authority financial resources are trivial compared to the legendary discretion wielded by Robert Moses through the Triborough Bridge and Tunnel Authority in New York from 1924 to 1968. There, easy access to toll revenue, combined with a lack of oversight (and a lack of available governance tools) from active owners and investors, led to spectacular failures of governance. In his authoritative biography, *The Power Broker: Robert Moses and the Fall of New York*, Robert Caro concisely describes the striking autonomy of the Triborough Bridge Authority and how Moses's virtually unchecked power was linked to an independent revenue source:

> Anyone who doubted Triborough's autonomy had only to look at its trappings. The empire had its own flag and great seal, distinctive license plates and a self-contained communications network, an elaborate teletype hookup that linked the [Triborough Authority headquarters] and the provincial capitals at Belmont Lake, Massena and Niagara.... [It] had its own fleets, of yachts and motorcars and trucks, and its own uniformed army—"Bridge and Tunnel Officers" who guarded its toll booths, revolver-carrying Long Island Parkway Police who patrolled its suburban parks and roads.... And, most significantly, it had its own source of revenue: the quarters and dimes that poured in a silver stream into the toll booths at which it collected tribute.[22]

Caro documents the enormous revenues of this unconstrained organization and the corrupting influence of those revenues in a framework uncontrolled by effective, activist ownership. Even the mayors and governors of New York were unable to impose any meaningful constraints on Moses's power. President Franklin Roosevelt tried, but even at the height of his popularity, he was unable to unseat Moses and ultimately retreated. Moses thus singlehandedly controlled vast wealth and power and was completely entrenched in his position—a deplorable governance failure due directly to the organizational form of a public-authority SOE.[23]

Whether or not such concentrated power in the hands of one person was ultimately good or bad for New York—a topic of much debate—is irrelevant for this discussion. What is clear is that the public-authority form of organization results in little oversight and control and vast discretion in the hands of one or a few managers, and thus poor governance. An arrangement in which the gains from such an organizational form depend on the beneficence, preferences, and predilections of any particular individual is not one that can be relied upon to produce social well-being over the long term. The use of firm resources to satisfy individual preferences would never be tolerated by active, private-sector owners and should not be tolerated by public-sector citizen-owners, either. These examples, which are not isolated, illustrate that the poorly defined property rights associated with an SOE create opportunities for individuals to gain control of those firms and exploit them for their own purposes, whatever they may be.

Critics may respond that governance failures at Enron, Tyco, World-Com, and other corporations were of equal, if not greater, concern. It is noteworthy, however, that those failures lasted for weeks or months—rather than for decades—as investors quickly withdrew capital when those failures became clear. Without investors' capital, corporations were rapidly restructured, went bankrupt, or were liquidated. SOE governance failures such as those described above can grind on for year after year, or even decade after decade, with the organization remaining essentially unchanged. This again stems from the lack of tradability of SOE residual claims, which prevents citizens from withdrawing their capital from failed and poorly governed enterprises.

Overall, this discussion illustrates the governance conundrum created by the political allocation of transportation spending. If allocated directly through the political process, transportation spending naturally becomes subject to political, rather than economic, forces. If, however, a state-owned enterprise (that is, a firm without shareholders) is used to manage those resources, by its very nature and design it is an independent agency and not subject to external checks and balances. Attempts to make SOEs "independent of politics" result in virtually unchecked managerial discretion. By injecting the monitoring and governance advantages of active shareholders, PPPs offer a way of cutting this Gordian knot, along with an array of additional advantages that I discuss in the following two chapters.

4

Benefits of PPPs:
Competition, Management,
and Project Delivery

The prevalence of private participation in many other U.S. network industries can help us appreciate the advantages of private participation in the transportation sector. In the electric utility industry, for example, as of January 1, 2008, private shareholders owned 55 percent of generating capacity, 61 percent of transmission capacity, and 52 percent of distribution capacity.[1] Similarly, natural gas, which flows through a network of high-pressure pipelines that function essentially as highways for gas, is distributed almost entirely through privately owned infrastructure. Natural gas is an enormously important utility in the United States, as it provides about 23 percent of all the marketable energy consumed.[2] Telecommunications is another example of a network industry in which the vast majority of the infrastructure is privately owned.[3] Equity holders in these industries obviously provide capital and bear risk, but they also inject incentives to take prudent risks, to operate the firm efficiently, to monitor managers rigorously, to innovate, and to focus on customer satisfaction to increase sales.

The same is true in transportation, where PPPs have the potential to convey an array of advantages for customers, taxpayers, and investors. I explore some of those benefits in this chapter and in the next and show how they are linked to the participation of private investors in designing, financing, constructing, maintaining, and operating valuable transportation facilities. In this chapter, I examine benefits stemming from greater competition, accelerated project delivery, stronger incentives for cost efficiency, and incentives to adopt new technologies.

PPPs Create Competition in Facility Management

A crucial advantage of PPPs is that they inject added competition into several segments of the transportation sector. Competition and private participation in the design-build segments are widely believed to have improved the provision of facilities and services over exclusive government provision. Increased use of PPPs allows the benefits of competition to be extended to the financing, management, and operation of transportation facilities.

Often unstated is that, without some type of private participation, government firms would have a de facto monopoly in the provision of transportation services.[4] Unregulated monopoly in the provision of any good or service creates social costs, even if the provider is a state-owned enterprise.[5] That is no less true in transportation than in any other sector. PPPs facilitate a special type of competition, however. Rather than bringing it only to firms within the transportation market itself, PPPs create competition for the right to finance, design, build, maintain, and operate transportation facilities. PPP-created competition occurs at the stage of bidding for a concession or design and construction contract, rather than continuously over time (as in most markets), although the threat of renegotiation and rebidding continues to discipline managers. Competition among firms for the right to serve a particular market—the prevailing term for which is *franchise bidding*—is a potent force whose importance has been recognized since at least 1859.[6] It was rediscovered in 1968 by Harold Demsetz and others, and today it has taken on renewed relevance in a variety of settings, including cable television.[7]

Franchise bidding can be structured in many different ways. When properly done, bidding for the right to serve a market can convey many of the advantages of competition within a market. With reference to a transportation facility, suppose bidding were to take place on the basis of the lowest toll acceptable to the concessionaire (unlike bidding for toll concessions on the Chicago Skyway or Indiana Toll Road, for example), with a predetermined lease term and clearly specified service-quality standards. In that case, if a sufficient number of firms bid for the right to serve a particular market, the toll would be bid down to the per-unit cost of providing the good or service.[8] Any unusual or "economic" profits would be squeezed out through the bidding process, and the winning firm would earn a normal rate of return—as in a competitive market.

A second advantage of franchise bidding is that it can achieve productive efficiency. A firm is said to be productively efficient if it is producing the maximum output it can with the inputs it uses while utilizing the best technology available. All else equal, if bidding is based on price as in many auctions—here for the lowest toll rate—then firms that are productively efficient will outbid those that are not because the franchise is most valuable to the most efficient firm. This is analogous to the outcome created by within-market competition, in which the most productively efficient firm (the one with the lowest price) wins increasing market share. Incentives to remain efficient and customer oriented are enhanced in ongoing operations by the threat that the franchise will be rebid—an important advantage of franchise bidding over traditional forms of regulation.[9]

Franchise bidding can be applied in other ways besides the lowest-toll approach, depending on the needs and desires of the public sponsor. For example, given a prespecified toll schedule and service-quality level, bidding can be based on the smallest net present value of revenue, with the concession rebid when that present value is received by the concessionaire.[10] Alternatively, given a preset toll schedule and level of service, bidding can take place on the basis of the shortest concession length. Regardless of the type of bidding used, these approaches all rely on PPPs to inject competition into the process of providing transportation services.

It is sometimes assumed that a large number of bidders is necessary to realize the benefits of PPP-induced competition. Up to some limit, more bidders will make the process more competitive. Even one unsolicited PPP bid, however, provides a benchmark against which the efficiency of sole public provision can be gauged. It also reveals information about which latest technologies are economically viable, as well as on what renovations and improvements private participants are willing to make. Such a bid also signals that a facility is PPP-viable, which may prompt public partners to undertake a more formal proposal process. For example, as discussed in chapter 2, an unsolicited bid to build HOT Lanes on the Capitol Beltway led the Virginia Department of Transportation to call for other proposals to build the HOT Lanes.

The process of comparing public- and private-sector provision of projects has been formalized in many countries under the rubric of "value for money," or VfM, analysis.[11] VfM is the concept—well-grounded in basic economics—that a privately financed option should not simply deliver lower cost, but rather should offer superior value per dollar spent compared to traditional public-sector procurement. That can include enhanced allocation of risk, faster project delivery, and more efficient maintenance, as well as lower construction and operating costs. An important element in comparing public- and private-sector delivery is the development of a detailed public-sector comparator, which reveals what it would cost the public sector to provide the outputs requested of the private sector under a traditional approach. A complete discussion of these concepts is outside the scope and purpose of this book. The critical point is that considering delivery via a PPP compels a careful comparison of the two approaches that would otherwise not take place and, thus, a new source of competition even if there is only one bidder.[12]

The benefits of PPP-induced competition also extend beyond the specific facility in question. Successful PPPs will make the sector more competitive overall. They serve as examples of the feasibility of competition for these services in the United States generally and show that it is possible for private managers and investors not only to design and build, but also to finance, expand, maintain, and operate transportation facilities. Fresh potential competition will affect the incentives of even those managers who do not face competition directly. This pressure will grow as more existing U.S. facilities are leased and as additional investor-operator partnerships gain sufficient expertise to bid on these projects.

PPPs Accelerate Project Delivery

One of the most compelling advantages of greater private participation in U.S. transportation is the ability to deliver critical projects more rapidly than under exclusive government provision. The National Surface Transportation Policy and Revenue Study Commission has identified slow project delivery as one of the most pressing problems facing the United States today:

Simply put, the Commission believes that it takes too long and costs too much to deliver transportation projects, and that waste due to delay in the form of administrative and planning costs, inflation, and lost opportunities for alternative use of the capital hinder us from achieving the very goals our communities set. Information compiled by the Federal Highway Administration (FHWA) indicates that major highway projects take approximately 13 years to advance from project initiation to completion (emphasis in original).[13]

Slow project delivery not only increases the cost of a project but also deprives motorists of transportation services and the latest technologies for the years or decades the project is delayed.

Private participation speeds project delivery for several reasons. Most obviously, PPPs provide access to a large pool of equity and debt capital unavailable under traditional debt-only financing approaches. This allows private partners to finance the often-massive upfront capital necessary to deliver projects quickly. "While lengthy development cycles are caused by multiple factors, not just funding gaps," the U.S. Department of Transportation states, "PPPs can help accelerate project delivery…by providing upfront capital to cover all of a project's costs."[14] Another U.S. Department of Transportation study reports that innovative contracting methods can reduce project durations by as much as 50 percent.[15] Additionally, PPPs that do not rely on federal funds can shorten project delivery times because they are not subject to the bureaucracy and red tape associated with federal funding. As Tom Skancke of the National Surface Transportation Policy and Revenue Study Commission testified in 2008, if you "add one federal dollar to a project, it adds 14 years to the delivery time."[16]

Another important reason for project acceleration is that private partners are motivated to get the deal done. Under traditional procurement, projects are sometimes held up for months or years due to haggling over environmental mitigation and transportation enhancements such as the installation of bike paths, sound walls, trees, and shrubs. Because private partners bear the cost of such delays, they are more likely to agree to such enhancements so the project can move forward. They also know that such enhancements will make the facility more attractive to customers, and that they will recapture at least some of the costs in higher revenue.

The incentives associated with private participation spur faster project completion generally, since active private participants will work hard to avoid losses stemming from delayed completion times. This is beneficial not only to the motorist-customers who obtain the facility's services sooner but also to the private participants; since "time is money," and because transportation construction costs have been rising faster than inflation generally, more rapid completion can save billions on large projects. In fact, the National Surface Transportation Policy and Revenue Study Commission stated that if the average development time for highway projects could be reduced from thirteen years to six, overall project costs could be reduced by almost 40 percent.[17] Those reductions can be passed on to investors in the form of cost savings, to citizens in the form of larger concession fees, or to motorists in the form of lower toll rates. They can also be passed on to citizens through the earlier realization of tax revenues (such as property, corporate, and taxable debt) associated with private participation, or through earlier revenue sharing. Some countries are consciously harnessing the power of incentives by, for example, including construction time in the overall concession term.[18] Since private partners cannot receive toll revenue until the facility is open to traffic, they are motivated to complete the facility quickly.

Moreover, transportation projects relying on private funding need not be subject to the vagaries of state budgetary processes, which can further slow project delivery. With private participation, whether or not a project proceeds is—or can be made—independent of the public sponsor's fiscal position at any particular time.[19] It is, instead, determined by the project's unique economic characteristics, such as revenue and cost. Indeed, if the project is privately funded by leveraging fees for road use, then the initial capital cost is largely a matter of concern to the private partner only.[20] Depending on anticipated revenues, private concessionaires are sometimes willing to pay taxpayers for the right to build facilities, so even new projects can, in some cases, improve states' budgetary situations. For example, a J. P. Morgan/Cintra partnership offered $2.8 billion to construct State Highway 121 in the Dallas region.[21] Revenue-sharing arrangements that would provide public sponsors with revenue over time are also possible.

The experience of other countries demonstrates that private financing allows projects to proceed that would otherwise languish. For instance, the Government Accountability Office tells us:

> Australian state governments have entered into highway public-private partnerships with private sector construction firms and lenders to finance and construct several toll highways in Sydney and Melbourne. Officials with the state of Victoria, Australia, have said that government preferences to limit their debt levels, particularly following a severe recession in the early 1990s, would have made construction of these roads difficult without private financing, even though some of the roads had been on transportation plans for several years.[22]

The ability of PPPs to raise the capital necessary to undertake projects has taken on renewed significance. Local governments have recently experienced difficulty in finding investors in municipal bonds. Unable to sell sufficient bonds and so to finance projects with debt, municipalities cannot undertake transportation projects.[23] Important projects have been canceled or delayed as a result.

Evidence indicates that PPPs do, in fact, expedite the completion of transportation projects, saving huge sums. For example, in its study of Australian PPPs, the Allen Consulting Group found that, on average, 3.4 percent of projects were completed ahead of time, while traditional projects were completed behind schedule 23.5 percent of the time.[24] As Ken Orski reports, the I-595 project in Florida, which will be done in five years with private participation, would have taken as long as fourteen years without it.[25] Similarly, San Diego's much-needed South Bay Expressway was built decades earlier than would have been possible without private participation.[26] And Ronald J. Daniels and Michael J. Trebilcock, referring to Highway 407 outside of Toronto, have written that

> although the provincial ministry of transport was initially committed to developing the project as a non-toll highway through the traditional procurement model, government budget constraints would have dictated the project's completion over

a twenty-year period. By structuring the project as a public/ private partnership, the government was able to expedite the project's development to four-and-a-half years.[27]

Recent assessments suggest that speeding project delivery is often the most compelling motivation for pursuing a PPP. "For new capacity projects," the National Surface Transportation Infrastructure Financing Commission reports,

> the public sector's primary motivation [for undertaking greenfield PPPs] is often accelerating delivery of a critical transportation project that has the potential to be self-financed at least in part through direct user fees or supported by specifically dedicated conventional revenues.[28]

As this discussion suggests, important projects are delayed for years and sometimes for decades because of governmental budget constraints, red tape, and bureaucracy. Numerous analysts have identified this as one of the most serious problems facing America's transportation sector today. As a growing body of evidence indicates, private participation speeds project delivery enormously by providing access to new capital, introducing powerful incentives, and streamlining bureaucratic processes. This is not accomplished at greater cost for a given level of facility quality, however. Rather, the PPP approach helps to contain costs, as I show in the following section.

PPPs Improve Incentives to Contain Costs and Efficiently Utilize Road Capacity

Private participants strive to earn profits. This impels the firm both to seek greater revenues and to lower costs. On the revenue side, given a capped toll rate, a private firm will work aggressively to increase throughput—that is, the number of motorists using a facility.[29] Revenue increases with the number of vehicles, up to the road's physical capacity. Since traffic delays mean less throughput and therefore less revenue, a private operator will do all it can to reduce delays. This implies that private firms will have a strong incentive to adopt congestion pricing, which is socially beneficial.[30] Congestion pricing is feasible on privately operated toll facilities and has so far been adopted on at least two major privately operated toll roads in North America: on Highway 407 north of Toronto and on the express lanes of State Route 91 in California. Examples exist in other countries as well.

Keeping the roadway clear at all times can also raise throughput. This involves quickly removing accidents, dead animals, debris, and obstructions, improving drainage, and keeping roadways free of ice and snow. Throughput can be further increased by widening bottlenecks and completing road repairs and refurbishments quickly and, to the extent possible, at off-peak times. Maximizing traffic volume is consistent both with motorists' desire to move swiftly and the social objective of using scarce transportation capacity wisely. Stated differently, and in sharp contrast to the status quo, private participation concentrates ownership in a group of people that bears directly the social cost of traffic delays via reduced revenues and has incentives to work hard to reduce them.

Second, a private firm need not take as given the number of motorists who wish to use a particular facility. Its goal of increasing revenues will motivate it to attract new customers. Most obviously, it can adopt a general customer-service orientation throughout its organization, creating an ethos of treating drivers, in fact, as customers rather than merely as "users." It can post customer-friendly websites that keep motorists informed of current congestion, construction, and weather conditions; it can advertise; it can adopt new, timesaving technologies, such as electronic toll collection; and it can maintain clean, safe rest areas and keep the facility aesthetically pleasing. The use of congestion pricing itself can attract new drivers as it reduces drivers' time costs and makes travel time more predictable, increasing the road's appeal.[31]

Private participation also affects cost. Private partners can take a number of actions to reduce costs, such as working aggressively to lower construction costs, subject to the contract's quality specifications. Faster project delivery also saves money, as noted earlier. One of the more important cost-saving measures stems from lifecycle management, also called lifecycle costing. This refers to a private partner's consideration of costs not only in the short term, but also over the entire life of its contract.

A firm is unlikely to defer spending on basic maintenance when it knows that it will likely incur much greater costs to restore deteriorated facilities—unlike governments, which often postpone basic maintenance of facilities. Lifecycle management thus lowers costs over a facility's life, giving private participants an incentive to adhere to a predetermined maintenance schedule.[32]

Private participation has resulted in significant overall savings, in transportation as well as other sectors. The United Kingdom's use of PPPs to obtain facilities such as hospitals, schools, and prisons was estimated to save 17 percent of costs compared to traditional procurement methods. These savings allow the public sector to deliver more projects and a higher quality of service than under traditional approaches.[33]

Critics sometimes argue that PPPs don't create any new revenue for transportation but are simply a different way of using a fixed amount of dollars. The above discussion reveals a few of the reasons why that view is wrong. The capital and incentives introduced by private participation encourage the operator to improve traffic throughput in many ways and to attract new customers, thus generating more revenue given a fixed toll and maintenance schedule on a particular facility. Those factors also allow providers to deliver a given level of service at lower cost. Importantly, higher revenues and lower costs simply reflect the greater social value the private operator is able to create from a facility through improved management techniques.

PPPs Improve Incentives to Enhance Safety

Although the above advantages of PPPs are compelling, the most salient benefit stemming from their use may be enhanced traffic safety. This is enormously important. Although U.S. traffic deaths have been declining, in 2008, 39,800 people were killed in U.S. traffic-related accidents. Even this huge number understates the social harm of traffic accidents (in terms of total life years lost) relative to other risks, such as cancer and heart disease, since accidents disproportionately affect young people. In 2007, for example, 3,174 teenage drivers were killed and nearly 252,000 teenage drivers were injured in auto crashes,[34] and while auto accidents ranked ninth in

2006 in terms of probability of death from all causes for all age groups, they ranked third in terms of expected life years lost.[35] Shockingly, in 2006, motor-vehicle crashes were the leading cause of death among Americans between the ages of four and thirty-four years. They were also the third leading cause of death (after congenital anomalies and accidental drowning) among toddlers ages one to three years.[36]

Everything possible must be done to reduce those staggering statistics. A for-profit firm has not only the necessary financial resources—obtained through its access to the capital markets—but also the high-powered incentives to do all it can to enhance the safety of the facilities it operates, since a reputation for hazardous travel has direct, dire financial consequences. This is not to suggest, of course, that government operators are unconcerned about safety, but rather that safety failures are unlikely to generate the same catastrophic institutional costs for a government as would be faced by a firm with a concentrated, well-defined group. Thus, a government does not confront the powerful incentives to be actively improving the safety of roadways that a private firms confronts. For a private firm, the financial effects of a poor safety record will also extend beyond immediate loss of traffic revenue to potential loss of the current concession and of future concessions on that and other facilities. In other words, the effects of a poor safety record on reputation are a matter of enormous concern to a private operator.

As a result, concessionaires will adopt all viable safety-enhancing measures as quickly as possible, and they have the financial resources to do so. Some of those resources may go toward the adoption of technology that improves safety, such as rumble strips on road shoulders and more numerous and stronger guard rails. A measure they could take in concert with the public officials who enforce speed limits is the installation of automatic radar devices, which have proved highly effective in reducing traffic fatalities in other countries. Newer safety-enhancing technologies include, among many other examples, the use of reflective paint containing tiny glass beads that make painted lines on highways more visible, particularly in the rain.

Using a PPP approach, such safety enhancements can be required by contract. For example, under the ultimately unconsummated agreement that Pennsylvania negotiated with Abertis/Citi to lease the Pennsylvania

Turnpike, the private partner would have had to implement a number of safety-enhancing road improvements, including fiber optics to detect accidents quickly. Similarly, when operations on the Indiana Toll Road were taken over by the Indiana Toll Road Concession Company, the concessionaire quickly installed barriers to prevent motorists from making dangerous U-turns using emergency vehicle crossovers.[37]

The amount and, importantly, the stability of funding for maintenance and improvements created by a PPP, combined with its incentives and contractual obligations, also enhance safety.[38] Since poorly maintained roads cause more accidents, deferred maintenance driven by governmental budget constraints erodes traffic safety—and the amount of deferred maintenance on America's roads is enormous. As of 2008, Pennsylvania alone needed an estimated $11 billion to address its deferred maintenance problem.[39] Under a PPP, road maintenance and repair are enforceable contractual requirements not subject to the vagaries of the political budgetary process.

The access to capital allowed by a PPP also delivers lifesaving new projects faster. New roads, bridges, and tunnels built and maintained with the latest accident-reducing technology are obviously much safer than outdated facilities. Even more obvious, a new limited-access, divided highway in an urban setting is safer per mile driven and will save more lives than a series of city streets where a motorist must traverse numerous intersections, each of which carries the risk of a deadly "T-bone" crash. A recent study concluded, for example, that the set of PPP highways that forms the almost-complete orbital (or beltway) system around Sydney, Australia, not only saves 38 million hours of travel time per year relative to a set of city streets, but also saves fifteen lives per year.[40]

The improved governance facilitated by a PPP also improves safety, since senior managers can be removed without a court proceeding if their facility systematically fails to meet safety goals. The threat of firing for poor safety performance is real. This contrasts sharply with governance under the current approach in which, as noted above, the governor of Massachusetts required court approval to remove the head of the Massachusetts Turnpike Authority after a fatal ceiling-tile collapse in Boston's "Big Dig" project.

Yet another way in which PPPs improve safety is that, as a result of their injection of substantial, fresh capital into transportation repair and renovation, they liberate public funds for other purposes. With the additional resources, law enforcement officials can better perform such core governmental functions as enforcing speed limits and drunk-driving laws, thus further lowering traffic fatalities.[41] Those liberated public funds also allow police officers and emergency medical services teams to respond more rapidly to accidents.

Finally, a private partner faces greater legal liability than a government operator. A private operator cannot be protected by sovereign immunity as embodied in the Eleventh Amendment of the U.S. Constitution, which typically protects states and their agencies.[42] States can, of course, affirmatively waive their agencies' sovereign immunity, so the degree of exposure to liability may vary by jurisdiction. Generally, though, exposure to tort liability is thought to induce more precaution and care, and this applies with particular force to the private operator, which therefore has stronger incentives than a government entity to ensure that its roadway is safe and maintained.[43]

PPPs Provide Incentives and Resources to Adopt Emerging Technologies

As the above discussion suggests, rapid technological adoption is an important advantage of private participation. New technology, in addition to being a boon to safety in the case of transportation PPPs, can lower costs while raising revenue by attracting additional customers. Electronic toll collection, for example, both raises revenue—because it saves time for motorists and increases throughput—and costs less than manned toll booths.

A revolution is currently under way in new technologies applicable to roads, bridges, tunnels, ports, and intermodal connectors. It extends far beyond simple electronic tolling, and I mention only a few of the many innovations here. One is the multifaceted system known as the intelligent transportation system, or ITS. ITS is a network of wireless and wire-line technologies that perform various transportation-related functions. One important dimension of ITS is vehicle-infrastructure integration, or VII, which uses dedicated short-range communications to allow vehicles to interact with nearby infrastructure and each other. The exchange of information on vehicle speed and orientation, among other variables, makes it possible to modify the speed and steering of properly equipped vehicles to avoid both roadway departures—one of the main causes of traffic fatalities—and collisions.[44] VII also allows vehicles to absorb information contained in roadway markings and signage and adjust accordingly. Finally, VII can improve the efficiency of road use by allowing vehicles to travel closer together without risk of collision.

Another example is the MEMS concrete monitoring system, developed by the engineering firm Advanced Design Consulting, which involves embedding a series of tiny sensors in freshly cast Portland cement.[45] The sensors can detect and report data (via a reader passed over the concrete) on the moisture, temperature, pH, chloride, sodium, and potassium ion content of the concrete throughout its service life. Facility managers thus have a much better picture of the overall condition of bridges or roadways, which is important for maintenance and safety. One can imagine the use of such sensors extended to other aspects of infrastructure, as well.

Similarly, a new device called an Electrochemical Fatigue Sensor, or EFS, is being developed.[46] This device reveals hard-to-detect cracks in metal and functions much like the electrocardiogram that tests the human heart. Originally developed for use in the aerospace industry, it can detect cracks down to a hundredth of an inch in size and assess how cracks change while a transportation facility, such as a bridge, is in use. It can also determine how a fracture is changing over time, which allows facility managers to focus on the most problematic deteriorations.

Of course, the development of such impressive new technologies does not ensure their adoption, but, once again, private firms are more likely to use them. Indeed, enhanced incentives to innovate are among the most consistently underappreciated benefits of private participation. Harvard economist Andrei Shleifer, for one, notes their importance.[47] In an influential survey article on government-owned versus privately owned firms, Shleifer emphasizes the weak incentives of public managers to innovate:

> When assets are publicly owned, the public manager has relatively weak incentives to make either of these investments [investments that either reduce costs or spur innovation or

quality improvement] because this manager is not the owner and hence gets only a fraction of the return. In contrast, private regulated contractors have much stronger incentives because, as owners, they get more of the returns on the investment. Which ownership structure is more efficient depends on whether having high-powered incentives to invest and innovate is a good idea.[48]

Transportation analysts appear to be in widespread agreement that high-powered incentives to invest and innovate are desirable in this sector. With respect specifically to transportation, the Government Accountability Office notes the link between incentives to adopt new technologies and the revenue-maximizing behavior that private participation introduces:

> In the case of the Chicago Skyway, the private concession company invested in electronic tolling technologies within the first year of taking over management of the Chicago Skyway. This action was taken because, in the long term, the up-front cost of new technologies would be paid off through increased mobility, higher traffic volumes, a reduced need for toll collectors, and decreased congestion at the toll plaza by increasing traffic throughput.[49]

All the evidence suggests that private participants have the resources, the willingness to take risk, and the incentives to adopt emerging technologies in this dynamic sector of the economy.

PPPs Improve Public Control over Assets

Aside from the added capital and better incentives they bring to facility operation, a major benefit of PPPs is that they improve citizen control over transportation assets for three main reasons.

First, as discussed in chapter 3, citizens' control over the transportation facilities they nominally own under current arrangements is very weak. This is partly due to the multiple levels of agency between the citizen-owners and the managers who ultimately run the facilities. If a state department of transportation operates a facility, for example, one agency problem may arise between citizens and their directly elected representatives, and another between those representatives and an appointee who heads the state department of transportation, and yet another between that department head and actual facility managers. A PPP reduces agency problems by allowing a team under the immediate control of a governor or mayor—which may include those directly elected officials—to negotiate clear performance standards with facility operators.

Second, a PPP replaces what may be vague or nonexistent maintenance, performance, and expansion standards with negotiated, transparent contractual control. The public partner can, for example, specify an array of observable performance criteria that the private partner must meet, such as rate of traffic flow, road surface quality, safety standards, maintenance standards, promptness of debris removal, and cleanliness of rest areas. Additional detailed performance metrics may include maximum values for the International Roughness Index,[50] the degree of obstruction of drainage systems, and the amount of pavement cracking, as well as minimum values for quality of signage, reflective paint, and tire adhesion. Some PPP contracts include hundreds of these performance criteria, termed key performance indicators.[51] Contracts can also specify the details of facility condition upon return to the public sponsor at the end of the concession period.

Maintenance standards are a particularly important PPP advantage because, as noted above, government entities may be tempted to defer maintenance during tight fiscal periods. Deferred maintenance is typically precluded by the terms of a PPP contract. Maintaining performance and customer service at a desirable level under the traditional approach is obviously difficult if benchmarks are never precisely defined. The clear performance and customer-service standards requisite to a PPP thus improve public—that is, citizen-owner—control over a facility.[52] "In contrast to commonly held perceptions about the relative transparency of PPPs," reports the Allen Consulting Group study of Australian PPPs, "we found that PPP projects were far more transparent than traditional projects, as measured by the availability of the public data for this study."[53] Indeed, the desired degree of public control can be adjusted based on the level of contractual detail.[54] If governments prefer greater control, they can write highly detailed contracts, and less detailed contracts if they believe greater control is unnecessary—subject to the constraint that potential investors are likely to place a lower value on a concession that requires them to accept a high degree of government intervention.

Existing PPP contracts illustrate this potential for control. The Indiana Toll Road contract holds the concessionaire to a higher level of performance than was required when the road was operated by the state. In fact, under government operation, the state did not have adequate funding to maintain the highway to its own standards, demonstrating the unenforceability of performance standards under government operation.[55] On the Chicago Skyway, the concessionaire must maintain and operate the facility according to industry best practices. The PPP agreement controls numerous dimensions of service quality, including safety features, roadway maintenance, drainage, toll-collection procedures, emergency planning, and snow removal. Surprisingly, no formal service or performance standards existed on the Skyway prior to the concession.[56]

The third way in which PPPs improve citizen control over transportation assets is through meaningful penalties for nonperformance, which facilitate effective contractual enforcement. With private participation, a monetary penalty is meaningful because, as stressed above, it will be paid by a concentrated, well-defined group of investors. The financial consequences of nonperformance to that group are clear, and it thus has strong incentives to ensure contractual standards are met. Similarly, managers' pay can be linked to clear performance metrics that provide incentives to meet defined standards.

In the case of the proposed lease of the Pennsylvania Turnpike, noncompliance with the terms of the contract—which was demanding and performance-based—would have allowed the Commonwealth of Pennsylvania to keep the entire concession fee and rebid the contract.[57] The ease of overseeing many dimensions of service quality on a transportation facility (such as snow removal, debris removal, road surface quality, and, with new technology, interior concrete quality) also facilitates contract enforcement, while private participation frees up resources, allowing the public sector to focus on enforcing performance standards.

In contrast, penalties for noncompliance with performance standards levied against a government toll authority or state department of transportation would lack credibility even if they existed. Such actions amount to government's levying a penalty on itself, which creates obvious conflicts of interest in enforcement. Moreover, there are no equity holders on whom the penalty can be assessed, so citizen-owners, rather than those who can actually control performance, inevitably pay. Such penalties are unlikely to have meaningful incentive effects.

The advantages of PPPs articulated here—greater competition, accelerated project delivery, more effective use of scarce road capacity, cost containment, enhanced safety, rapid technological adoption, and improved public control—are impressive. However, they ignore the benefits accruing to key participants—the investing public—as well as critical functions those participants provide by assuming risks inherent in the financing, construction, maintenance, and operation of major transportation facilities. I turn next to exploring these benefits.

5

Benefits of PPPs:
Investment, Risk Transfer, and the
Rationalization of Investment

In this chapter, I focus on advantages PPPs convey to an important but sometimes neglected group: the investors who enjoy new opportunities as a result of PPPs. I first discuss why it is critical to introduce new groups of investors to fund infrastructure, and then I review the benefits of PPPs to those investors themselves. I follow by examining several extant policies that help encourage private participation in infrastructure investment. I then consider two important social benefits that investors provide: the assumption of risk and the rationalization of transportation investment.

PPPs Introduce New Classes of Investors

Most obviously, PPPs allow entirely new groups of investors—rather than simply the limited pool of municipal bond investors—to fund transportation infrastructure. This is important because bonds are an inherently conservative method of finance that promises timely, fixed repayment of principal plus interest to bondholders. Because payments are fixed, bondholders receive no additional return if a project performs well. Their focus is on minimizing the risk of default. Since a bond-only financing arrangement by definition provides no equity cushion to shield bondholders from potential losses, they will demand security through other means. One is to require the debt-coverage ratio—the percentage by which revenues generated by an asset must exceed debt payments—to be relatively high.[1] To obtain an investment-grade rating, municipal bonds typically must have annual revenues between 25 percent and 100 percent *more* than the cost of annual debt service.[2] This gives bondholders the financial cushion that equity would otherwise create, but it also mechanically limits the amount of capital that can be raised using bond financing for a given amount of toll revenue.

Equity investment thus raises more capital not only through the additional supply of funds to which it has access, but also indirectly through the financial cushion it offers bondholders, which facilitates a lower debt-coverage ratio.[3] The greater tolerance for risk associated with equity investment also allows for less conservative forecasts of revenue growth, and thus more upfront value for citizens. For example, in its final report, the National Surface Transportation Infrastructure Financing Commission stated,

> Equity investors are generally willing to "underwrite" higher growth rates than will debt investors. While the debt markets will assume minimal (and sometimes zero) growth of net revenues, equity participants are willing to contemplate much higher growth rates in their forecasts of return and take the associated risks.[4]

Compared to many other countries, the United States is an appealing place for equity investment in infrastructure. One important reason for this is its tradition of effective contract enforcement. Contract enforcement is critical under a PPP arrangement, in which investors require credible, long-term assurances that the government will not expropriate their investment. This is consistent with the observation that infrastructure projects are generally more successful in developed countries, where contractual enforcement is robust.[5] A large body of careful research also suggests that countries with a predominantly common-law tradition, such as the United States, have better protections for minority investors, and thus better-developed capital markets.[6]

By including equity investors as well as new types of bond investors, PPPs directly and significantly increase the pool of funds available for transportation infrastructure.[7] Increased use of PPPs would allow billions of dollars in fresh capital to flow into U.S. transport construction and renovation, bringing the benefits not only of rejuvenated infrastructure but also of new opportunities for patient, prudent investors. As some investors are likely to be from other countries, I next address concerns arising from their involvement. This is correctly referred to as global investment, as I show below.

Global Investment in U.S. Transportation Infrastructure

Participation in transportation by global investors and operating companies should be welcomed and encouraged in the United States. Investors from around the world bring fresh capital and high-powered incentives that will renew American infrastructure. Global construction and operating companies bring decades of knowledge and experience to facility operation while making the PPP bidding process much more competitive. Vague concerns are sometimes expressed, however, about granting "foreign" investors "control" over critical transportation assets. Such a concern is difficult to understand as anything other than an attempt to undermine PPPs by playing on xenophobia. Global investment in and management of U.S. transportation infrastructure should be encouraged rather than hindered for at least five reasons.

First, and perhaps most obviously, transportation assets are by their nature sunk and cannot be physically expropriated by any investor, no matter where they are located.[8] Since global investors are investing in fixed U.S. assets, they are assuming the sovereign risk that the relevant state or local government will fail to adhere to contractual terms and will take some action—such as eliminating tolls—that reduces the value of their investment. This key point has been subject to so much misinformation that Americans might well think they were the ones assuming sovereign risk. On discussions surrounding the proposed lease of the Pennsylvania Turnpike after Abertis/Citi's $12.8 billion offer, state representative Rick Geist, the Republican cochair of the House Transportation Committee in Pennsylvania, commented, "The misinformation was almost to the point that people thought the Spaniards were going to take the highway and move it back to Spain."[9]

Second, capital movements today do not recognize international borders. Markets are highly globalized and becoming more so over time.

Simply because the home base of an investment fund is Australia, Portugal, or Spain does not imply that the actual investors in those funds are based there. For example, 47 percent of the investors in one Australian infrastructure fund, Macquarie Infrastructure Partners, are from the United States.[10] Those American investors include construction trade unions such as the Midwest Operating Engineers Pension Fund and the Mid-Atlantic Carpenters Pension Fund, among others. The distinction between "foreign" and "domestic" investors thus lacks substance. Moreover, as this example illustrates, the term "foreign investment" is itself a misnomer since investment funds—wherever based—necessarily include American investors due to the depth of U.S. capital markets. Global investment is thus the correct term.

Indeed, if PPP critics successfully precluded investment in U.S. transportation infrastructure based on an investment fund's country of origin, they would be denying U.S. pension funds, university endowments, and others those investment opportunities. Given the intensity of global competition for infrastructure investment, they would effectively be forcing those U.S. funds and endowments to invest in transportation infrastructure in other countries—surely an undesirable outcome, given America's desperate need for infrastructure investment.

Third, as I have emphasized, ultimate control always remains with the public partner. Investors have no ability to interfere with any broader public uses of the facility, including such national security needs as moving military vehicles. Clauses can be included in PPP agreements specifying that any national security use of the facility overrides commercial use, binding investors of any national origin by the same contractual requirements. Moreover, a large body of federal law exists to address any national security issues raised by foreign investment.[11]

Fourth, long experience suggests that global participation in infrastructure is not a cause for concern. Foreign-based companies have been operating critical U.S. infrastructure for decades, with no ill effects on national security or any other social goal. Foreign companies currently operate U.S. ports, airports, and water and wastewater plants as well as highways, and provide expert management and operational skills in all those areas. For example, foreign companies run 80 percent of the terminals at the country's busiest port, the Port of Los Angeles, and foreign firms or their subsidiaries operate terminals at seven of the ten busiest U.S. cargo ports.[12] A domestic subsidiary of a French-owned company, Veolia, provides the water supply for Indianapolis.

Finally, I have emphasized that transportation PPPs are relatively new to the United States, at least in the modern era. The most investment experience and operational expertise thus lies overseas by default.[13] If the United States wishes to enjoy the latest technology and management methods available, it must welcome global investors and operating companies. Even if U.S. facility-operating companies in fact possessed decades of experience, global participation would still be beneficial for the increased competition it brings to the PPP process. I next discuss the benefits of infrastructure investments to a critical group: the investors themselves.

PPPs Offer Investors New Options

The prevailing vehicles for infrastructure investment, such as direct participation in a PPP or the purchase of an unlisted fund, are most accessible to large investors. Those investors include such entities as public and private pension funds, insurance companies, mutual funds, and university endowments. I focus here on such large investors.

The traditional approach, which often funds infrastructure using tax-exempt debt under traditional procurement methods, offers little opportunity for tax-exempt pension funds and nonprofits to benefit from infrastructure investing; they would simply receive a lower interest rate with no concomitant tax benefit. Thus, only infrastructure that is financed at least partly through private debt and equity participation offers these large investors the opportunity to invest in transportation facilities while anticipating returns consistent with their fiduciary duties.[14]

Such investors may also find the predictable cash flows typically generated by transportation infrastructure investments to be a good match with their long-term liabilities. Although certainly not immune to economic fluctuations, cash flows generated by transportation facilities are stable relative to many other sectors, which will help pension funds, insurance companies, and others remain sound through difficult financial periods. For example, according to the Dow Jones Brookfield Global

Infrastructure Index, the median EBITDA[15] growth of infrastructure companies was positive in 2008 and 2009, while the S&P 500 index suffered steep declines over the same period.[16] Infrastructure is also appealing because it offers the chance to invest in something tangible and long lasting and, in fulfilling a critical social need, is consistent with socially responsible investing.[17] At a minimum, infrastructure investments provide investors with additional portfolio diversification opportunities. To the extent that toll caps are indexed to inflation, cash flows are also protected against inflation.[18]

Commentators sometimes debate the amount of private investment available to fund U.S. infrastructure. Certainly, all of the institutional investors mentioned above control substantial assets, so even relatively small allocations to transportation infrastructure will result in large absolute amounts available for facility construction and renovation.[19] The amount of capital potentially available for U.S. infrastructure investment, however, depends on conscious policy choices. If proposals such as that for the creation of a federal Office of Public Benefit—which would generate an unnecessary new layer of bureaucracy to exercise more centralized control over proposed state-level PPPs—are adopted, then uncertainty will increase, reducing investment.[20] Conversely, if more facilities and lanes are tolled, then those cash-generating facilities are likely to attract more investment. If additional states adopt PPP-enabling legislation, then they are likely to see greater private investment in infrastructure.[21] If the advantages of the PPP approach are thoughtfully explained to the public and the public becomes more accepting of PPPs, more investment will be attracted.

Large institutional investors have, indeed, recognized the benefits of infrastructure investing.[22] According to Probitas Research, infrastructure equity funds raised $34.3 billion globally in 2007 and $24.7 billion in 2008.[23] As of early 2009, seventy new funds were in or coming to the infrastructure market, and vendors in that market were seeking investments of over $92 billion.[24] As of March 2010, over thirty infrastructure funds were prepared to invest in the United States with a levered investment potential of $475 billion.[25] The total amount of investment dedicated to infrastructure has also grown rapidly, tripling from 2006 to 2009. Public pension funds provide 45.6 percent of the investment in infrastructure equity funds, while insurance companies provide about 36 percent.[26]

Australia is the international leader in infrastructure allocations and actual investment. Australian pension (or superannuation) funds invest approximately 5 percent of their assets in infrastructure, with some investing considerably more.[27] Outside of Australia, funds dedicate smaller fractions of their investments to infrastructure. A 2008 survey showed that the average infrastructure allocation of pension funds in the United Kingdom was only 0.8 percent on an asset-weighted basis, with allocations only marginally higher in continental Europe.[28] U.S. infrastructure investment activity is in the early stages, but interest appears to be growing. The massive California Public Employees Retirement System (CalPERS), for example, adopted a target infrastructure investment allocation of 3 percent in 2008.[29] Generally, small international allocations suggest that, although the dollar amounts mentioned above are large, considerable room remains in this area for commitment growth.

Commitments include a range of infrastructure types. Regarding transportation investment specifically, the total number of PPP highway projects planned and funded globally between 1985 and 2009 was 1,046, valued at $580 billion.[30] Unfortunately, the United States accounts for a much smaller proportion of those totals than Europe: only 77 U.S. highway PPP projects, valued at $84.6 billion, were planned and funded during that time. Given the size of its economy, its investment needs, and its history of reliable contract enforcement, the United States is ideally positioned to attract more private participation.

A number of vehicles are available for investing in infrastructure. Both debt and equity interests can be purchased. Although bank loans dominate on the debt side of financing, larger infrastructure companies do issue bonds. On the equity side, one straightforward approach is to purchase either listed or unlisted equity in an infrastructure company such as Transurban or Leighton Holdings.

Investors can also participate directly in a particular PPP. For example, in 2009 the Dallas Police and Fire Pension System acquired a 10 percent stake in the $2.7 billion Texas LBJ Freeway PPP.[31] While direct PPP participation may be appropriate for large, sophisticated investors who can devote substantial resources to such efforts, it may be outside the scope and expertise of others. It is also less likely to be liquid and may provide less diversification across projects and therefore greater exposure to regulatory and project-specific risks, unless investors are large enough to assemble a broad set of projects. Despite these challenges, the direct approach appears to be gaining appeal globally.[32]

Another avenue is to purchase equity in either a listed or an unlisted infrastructure fund. Unlisted funds are illiquid compared to listed funds, but they tend to reflect better the risk/reward characteristics of the under-lying infrastructure asset. They also provide diversification across projects.[33] Since equity in a listed fund can be purchased directly on a stock exchange, it is more liquid and provides direct access to expert-managed infrastructure investing, but, in part because of its liquidity, it is more affected by general equity-market movements. Its behavior is thus likely to be closer to that of traditional equity than to that of an unlisted fund. Other investment decisions include whether to focus on domestic versus international investments, among others.[34]

As U.S. infrastructure investment matures as an asset class, more (and simpler) investment options, such as infrastructure index funds, are likely to emerge. Indeed, other options, including private-equity funds, exchange-traded funds, and arrangements akin to real estate investment trusts, are emerging.[35]

PPPs Transfer Risk from Taxpayers to Professional Risk Bearers

Another reason to encourage private infrastructure investment stems from the ability of private investors to bear many of the important risks associated with the financing, design, construction, renovation, and operation of any transportation facility. Specific risks vary with the project in question. Examples include those brought about by changes in traffic volume (and thus revenues), changes in the cost of repair and renovation, labor disputes, *force majeure* risks (that is, risks associated with such exogenous events as earthquakes, wars, floods, and tidal waves), and legal liability risks, as well as regulatory and political risks arising from changes in government policy, risks from requirements for environmental permits related to facility construction or expansion, risks associated with design failure, and risks of the construction of competing public and private facilities, among many others. Construction risks, most important for new facilities, include cost and time overruns, unexpected geological challenges, and construction hazards.[36]

These risks exist regardless of whether a project is delivered through traditional procurement or a PPP. They are inherent in the particular project. One of the key benefits of PPPs, however, is that they allow some risks to be transferred from citizen-owners to private participants through contractual specifications. This is a valuable benefit, and real risks have, indeed, been transferred to private-sector partners in a number of projects. The CityLink project in Melbourne, Australia, for example, encountered numerous difficulties during construction, including problematic geological conditions and a tunnel failure, which resulted in much higher costs and project delays. Those additional costs were not borne by the Victorian government, since the contract assigned them to the concessionaire.[37]

Traffic or revenue risk is particularly important for greenfield PPPs since expected traffic flows can only be inferred using statistical modeling, while traffic flows on brownfield PPPs are known.[38] The Camino Columbia Toll Road (CCTR) around Laredo, Texas, illustrates the importance of greenfield traffic risk and thus the value of transferring that risk from taxpayers to investors. The CCTR is a twenty-two-mile-long connection between I-35 in Texas and the principal highway to Monterrey, Mexico.[39] It cost approximately $90 million to construct and was opened to traffic in October 2000. The original plan was to charge cars $3.00 and trucks $16.00 to use the road. Traffic forecasts predicted 300 cars and 1,500 trucks per day, which would have generated $9 million in annual revenue. Although the number of cars was underpredicted, the expected number of trucks never materialized. Actual truck traffic was 75 per day, with annual revenue of only $500,000. Truckers continued using Bridge 4 in Laredo, which also linked to I-35. The CCTR was sold at a foreclosure auction in 2004 for $12 million and was later acquired by the Texas Department of Transportation for $20 million.[40] In the end, citizens gained ownership of a virtually new facility at a highly discounted price.

The financial failure of a particular transport PPP is sometimes viewed as a failure of the PPP approach generally. That conclusion does not follow. No one would seriously contend, for example, that because one steel company failed, funding steel companies with private capital was somehow a flawed model. Instead, the willingness to accept risk (which, by definition, implies occasional failure) in order to discover economically viable investments should be lauded.

In the CCTR case, private-equity participants were willing to accept voluntarily the known risks inherent in financing and constructing the new transport facility. The number of customers was necessarily uncertain because the facility was not yet built. This situation is analogous to the launching of a new product by an entrepreneur. Before the product is launched, the entrepreneur can only rely on educated guesses as to how many customers will buy it. Some products will be financial failures, while others will be resounding successes. Everyone benefits from having entrepreneurs offer new, innovative products, even if some fail.

Just as an entrepreneur provides a social benefit by assuming the risk of trying new products (and thus revealing which are most desirable), the PPP approach generates the social benefit of allowing professional risk takers to offer innovative transportation facilities. Under the PPP approach in the CCTR case, investors' assumption of traffic risk meant that it did not have to be assumed by taxpayers. But, perhaps more important, private participation allows risks to be taken in constructing new facilities that would otherwise never be built—that is, equity participation results in more risk taking overall.

This discussion suggests that, in addition to supplying capital for facility construction and renovation, investors should be thought of as providing citizens with risk-bearing services. Risk is spread among many large, diversified investors who assume it voluntarily, rather than being borne by taxpayers who are not compensated directly for accepting it and who may be poorly diversified and risk averse.[41] In many countries, risk sharing is seen as an important benefit of PPPs. Darrin Grimsey and Mervyn K. Lewis tell us that "although governments have been motivated into entering into PPP agreements by the desire to reduce debt (and contain taxation), another consideration has been the benefits of sharing financial risks and rewards between public and private sector bodies."[42] Underscoring the importance of risk transfer, both Spain and Portugal conduct feasibility analyses prior to entering into PPPs. A project is likely to proceed if the analysis concludes that a large portion of the project's risk can be transferred to the private sector.[43]

One of the main functions of a PPP agreement, then, is to allocate risks between citizens and the private partner.[44] An obvious question follows: which risks are best borne by investors and which by citizens in their capacity as owners? Investors may be better able to manage some risks (that is, to bear them at lower cost), while others are best borne by government. Careful consideration of this question is critical for attaining optimal risk transfer via the PPP contract.[45]

PPP risks have been usefully divided into two broad categories: global risks and elemental risks.[46] Global risks include legal, environmental, and political risks, while elemental risks arise from operational, financial, and revenue-generation issues. The public partner may, for example, be better able to manage risks associated with environmental permitting and political events, whereas private partners are better positioned to manage elemental risks and spread them out over many diversified investors. The parties can and should, however, determine through negotiation the best allocation of risk for themselves, which can then be reflected in contractual terms—in other words, there is no one best risk allocation, as the optimal risk allocation will, in general, vary across projects and jurisdictions.[47] Moreover, the public sponsor may wish to assume greater risk to attract private investment and to realize other benefits associated with private participation. Daniels and Trebilcock point out, for example, that on the Prince Edward Island Fixed Link project in Canada, the government assumed numerous exogenous risks, such as delays related to government regulation, war, earthquakes, nuclear events, and environmental injunctions, among others.[48]

Private Participation Reveals the True Cost of Capital

This discussion of risk bearing sheds light on an important aspect of the PPP debate. Public financing is sometimes said to be cheaper because of the government's unique taxing power. Experts now recognize that government provision does not result in a lower cost of capital, but instead results in a mispricing of the risk assumed by citizen-owners. For example, after many years of experience with PPPs of various types, John Pierce, the secretary of the New South Wales Treasury in Australia, stressed,

It is a myth that governments have access to "cheaper" finance to undertake projects—a government's ability to borrow more cheaply is purely a function of its capacity to levy taxes to repay borrowings. Credit markets (rightly) perceive this coercive power as reducing the risk of their investment, and are therefore willing to lend to a government at lower rates than to a private sector borrower.

However, when it comes to raising finance for a project on a non-recourse basis, it is the risk of the individual project that determines the real cost of finance.

The difference between the private and the public sectors is that private capital markets explicitly price in the risk of a project into its sources of finance. This is not the case in the public sector. Instead, taxpayers implicitly subsidize the cost of a project by bearing the risk of cost overruns, time delays or performance failures, which are not priced into the government borrowing rate.[49]

Like many other problems, mispricing of risk stems from the lack of tradability of citizens' residual claims. Citizens' ownership interest in a transportation facility is tied to their residence in a particular jurisdiction. Since citizens have no right to sell their equity shares in state-owned enterprises, scholars refer to them as captive equity holders.[50] If those claims were tradable, claimants would have to be compensated for the risk they bear or else they would withdraw their capital. Indeed, private participation helps address the mispricing problem by making the cost of risk assumption clear in the bid price.[51]

This discussion also exposes the fallacy inherent in any analysis comparing PPPs with the traditional approach that considers citizen-owners' equity to be a "free" input.[52] Any "savings" from the failure to pay citizen-owners a market rate of return is a savings only in the same sense that the failure to pay a market wage to captive workers represents a savings. Similarly, the use of government power to expropriate materials for facility construction at a below-market rate cannot properly be counted as a savings from government operation.

Surprisingly, state governments have, in fact, used captive labor as well as captive equity to build roads. For example, before the 1790s, the State of New York assessed eligible males a minimum of three days of roadwork per year under penalty of fines.[53] No legitimate policy analysis would count the wages "saved" from such forced labor as an advantage of government provision. A market wage (the opportunity cost of workers' time and energy) must be imputed instead. Similarly, a market rate of return on equity capital must be imputed in any legitimate comparison of the costs of public versus private provision of a transportation project.

As with any business, paying equity investors a return on capital to draw that capital to a project or activity is a true production cost, just as paying workers a wage sufficient to attract their labor and paying the prevailing price for materials are true production costs. To the extent that government firms do not pay citizens a return on their capital invested, an implicit subsidy stems from their status as captive equity holders. The same implicit subsidy occurs when taxpayers are captive equity holders in other state-owned enterprises, such as the U.S. Postal Service, the Tennessee Valley Authority, the Bonneville Power Authority, Amtrak, and many others.

Making the actual cost of risk assumption transparent also helps rationalize infrastructure investment, since it is a true cost that must be counted in any assessment of a project's net economic benefits. Inclusive of the cost of risk, some projects may not be self-supporting. I discuss the role of PPPs in rationalizing transportation investment in more detail below.

PPPs Rationalize Transportation Investment

The core of the standard real-toll PPP approach is an enforceable contract that requires a facility to be operated, maintained, and expanded according to detailed, observable specifications. Prior to entering into a contract, investors consider carefully whether the tolls paid by motorists to use a particular facility—that is, aggregate "willingness to pay," or aggregate customer value—will be sufficient to cover the cost of all inputs, including a market, risk-adjusted rate of return on capital invested. Investors will proceed only if anticipated toll revenue is sufficient to cover those costs.

This has important implications. As noted in chapter 1, one of the most pressing problems facing America's transportation system today is the diversion of monies paid by motorists, usually through fuel taxes, to projects that are driven by politics rather than by the value they create for motorists. Careful assessment of the benefits to motorists and the costs of a project by private participants prior to construction helps avoid wasteful projects. Scholars have recognized this. According to Eduardo Engel, Ronald Fischer, and Alexander Galetovic,

> In stark contrast to public provision, the BOT [build-operate-transfer] scheme uses the market mechanism instead of central planning to screen projects. This helps prevent building white elephants, as no private firm wants to franchise a road that will make it lose money, where a white elephant is defined as a project whose net (of costs) social value is negative.[54]

As also noted by Efriam Sadka, "In this context [where costs and benefits are hard to determine] PPPs may play a useful role in enhancing a proper cost-benefit analysis and reducing the likelihood of building 'white elephants,' such as a multilane highway that runs from nowhere to nowhere."[55] By reducing such wasteful projects, PPPs help rationalize transportation investment.

In this way, private participation interacts with the price signals that help guide investment, as discussed at the end of chapter 1. It is thus not sufficient for price signals simply to exist. For investment actually to flow to where it is valued most, suppliers must have both the capital and the incentives to act on those signals. Private participation provides both.

Another way in which PPPs help to rationalize investment is distinct from the decision about whether to build a particular facility. A PPP introduces a legally enforceable, ongoing link between the toll revenue motorists provide and the expenditures to operate, maintain, and expand a facility—that is, a PPP ensures that, once a facility is built, monies spent by motorists to use it will remain with that facility. PPPs thus reduce revenue diversion.

Realistic *ex ante* cost-benefit project assessment plays another valuable social role. It reveals which parts of the system are self-sustaining and which are not. Such information is enormously valuable because it provides the foundation for rationalizing transportation spending. Those facilities that are self-sustaining can—and should—be provided through an unsubsidized PPP. This is perhaps the purest form of the user-pays principle that originally motivated the fuel-tax approach.

This point begs the question of how much of the surface transportation system is potentially self-sustaining. It may seem that PPPs would be profitable only on a small set of facilities. Studies indicate, however, that profitable private operation of toll facilities is feasible in a wide range of settings, including on urban roads and when reasonable price regulation is implemented.[56] PPPs could thus likely operate without subsidies on a wider range of facilities than many commentators realize.

Although I do not examine the question in detail here, some facilities and system parts that are not self-sustaining may be socially desirable for other sound policy reasons (rather than simply political appeal). This, of course, does not mean that the facilities cannot be priced, but, rather, that they require subsidies to operate.[57] PPPs can play an important role even for these facilities if the nature of bidding is changed. Here, private investors would bid for the right to construct or operate a facility based on the smallest acceptable subsidy rather than on the largest concession fee, the lowest toll, or some other criterion. The private partner who bids the lowest subsidy wins. This approach has the key advantage of ensuring that the subsidy is delivered in the most efficient manner possible—that is, it ensures that the public receives the greatest value per dollar of subsidy. This method of bidding for highway projects has been used in Spain and Canada and could easily be extended to other venues.[58]

Additionally, shadow tolls or availability payments can be used to supplement actual toll revenues on a low-use facility to make private participation feasible—that is, a mixture of real tolls, shadow tolls, and availability payments can be used, with the subsidy delivered through the shadow tolls and availability payments. The mix can be changed over time—for instance, projects whose traffic volume early on is insufficient to support a PPP using only real tolls can begin with a combination of real and shadow tolls and/or availability payments, and then phase out the subsidy as traffic volume rises. That approach is being considered in Portugal.[59] All these ways of delivering a subsidy have the advantage of preserving the range of benefits PPPs provide, including innovative and timely project delivery, risk assumption, competition, investment opportunities, lifecycle management, and improvement of public-asset control through contracts.

Given all these possibilities, public policies should be structured to facilitate the process of revealing the most economical parts of the transportation system by encouraging PPPs. This helps to increase the transparency of any cross subsidies. One way to do this is to facilitate unsolicited PPPs. Some state PPP-enabling laws allow this. The California Department of Transportation, for one, invited private firms to submit toll road project proposals, which it would then evaluate.[60] Below I discuss several other policies states and localities can pursue to encourage private infrastructure investment.

Public Policies to Encourage Infrastructure Investment

I close this chapter by discussing public policies that promote private infrastructure investment. I first discuss two general policies that will improve the institutional environment in which PPPs operate, and thus facilitate private participation: creating policy predictability and lowering transaction costs. I then describe four existing policies that encourage private investment. Those include PPP-enabling state legislation, private activity bonds, TIFIA loans, and state infrastructure banks.

Policy Predictability and Regulatory Certainty. Perhaps the single most important general policy facilitating private investment is to provide a stable institutional environment that reduces uncertainty and allows investors to plan for the long term. "Institutional environment" refers to the full set of laws, norms, and regulations affecting the returns on infrastructure investment. It includes stability of property rights and contracting arrangements surrounding the design, construction, and operation of the facility, as well as a stable regulatory environment. Policy predictability requires the government to be consistent in its treatment of private investment over time.[61] If, for example, the government announces that it will not use regulations to depress tolls below the costs of facility operation, it must remain committed to that policy. A stable institutional environment will not only attract investment, but also drastically lower capital costs, since investors need not factor in uncertainty associated with changes in government behavior.

Reduce Transaction Costs. Transaction costs are very broad in nature. They include the cost of bidding and negotiating the agreement, of actually writing up the contract, and of monitoring and enforcing the agreement. Any approach that relies on contracting with a private firm, such as a simple design-build contract, will incur transaction costs.[62] A greater level of private participation, such as through a DBFO (design, build, finance, and operate) contract, implies more complex contracting as well as longer-term monitoring of contractual compliance.

Reducing transaction costs lowers the overall social costs of the PPP approach. It also entices more bidders to participate, which increases the level of competition at the bidding stage. There are several ways that public policy can reduce transaction costs. As noted above, providing a stable legal and policy environment for a PPP will reduce uncertainty, leaving private participants less in need of contractual clauses protecting their investments from this type of sovereign risk. Contract standardization can also reduce transaction costs by minimizing uncertainty and making it simpler to compare bids, which is another aspect of completing the transaction. Other actions focus on keeping the process competitive by directly reducing the substantial costs of bidding. One scheme that has been used in Canada is to have the winning bidder use project proceeds to pay an honorarium to losing bidders.[63]

State PPP-Enabling Laws. Another approach to encouraging investment is to pass state PPP-enabling laws. These laws streamline the PPP process in a state and eliminate the need for the legislature to act to complete a PPP. They typically include provisions that

- give explicit authority to the state, usually through an agent (such as the state department of transportation), to enter into PPP agreements;

- specify whether unsolicited PPP bids are allowed;

- specify whether state, local, and federal funds can be combined with private funds to finance the project;

- clarify where rate-setting authority rests;

- specify whether the overall number of PPP projects is limited; and

- clarify a number of other aspects of state policy with respect to PPPs.

As of March 2010, twenty-eight states had enacted PPP-enabling laws.[64] The laws help attract private-sector investment because, among other factors, they reduce transaction costs, and they signal a state commitment to utilizing PPPs. State-level PPP activity is also important for its ability to teach states about the best way to approach PPPs. States can try different PPP approaches and learn from one another's experience. Learning by doing is critical in realizing the full benefits of private participation.

Private Activity Bonds (PABs). In 1986, the federal Tax Reform Act replaced existing industrial development bonds with a new category of tax-exempt bonds called "private activity bonds," or PABs.[65] PABs are a municipal–corporate finance hybrid. They are tax-exempt bonds issued by or on behalf of local or state governments in order to provide special financing benefits to qualified projects (even though the government generally does not pledge its credit). The proceeds of the bond issue are usually used by one or more private entities, and the bonds are paid off solely through project-generated revenues and other privately provided security. Under this arrangement, the municipality is effectively lending its tax-exempt status to a private firm participating in a qualifying project. Municipalities examine such projects carefully because their names are on the bonds and their credit ratings may be affected.

In recognition of the potential application of PABs to transportation, the 2005 Safe, Accountable, Flexible, Efficient Transportation Equity Act: A Legacy for Users (SAFETEA-LU) authorized the U.S. secretary of transportation to allocate up to $15 billion in PABs for qualified transportation projects. Additionally, SAFETEA-LU amended the Internal Revenue Code to add bridge, highway, and intermodal freight facilities to the types of private projects for which PABs can be issued.[66] The American Recovery and Reinvestment Act of 2009 encouraged PAB use by exempting them from the alternative minimum tax.[67] A $15 billion cap remains, however, on the total amount of PABs that can be issued.

Advantages of PABs include stimulating private investment in infrastructure by lowering borrowing costs and allowing tax-exempt debt to be combined with equity investment. Indeed, PABs "effectively eliminate the differential in interest costs between debt issued by the public and private sectors."[68] This will encourage added private investment, which is prudent given the range of social benefits associated with private participation outlined above.[69] As of January 2010, the U.S. Department of Transportation had approved almost $6.3 billion in PAB allocations. Almost $1 billion worth was issued for the Capital Beltway HOT lanes and the North Tarrant Expressway in Texas.[70]

Transportation Infrastructure Financing and Innovation Act (TIFIA) Loans. TIFIA is a credit-assistance program created as part of the Transportation Equity Act for the 21st Century (TEA-21), enacted in June 1998 and expanded in SAFETEA-LU in 2005. Administered by the U.S. Department of Transportation, its purpose is to provide credit assistance to major transportation projects—that is, projects of national or regional significance. Assistance can take the form of lines of credit, direct loans, or loan guarantees. According to the U.S. DOT, "The program's fundamental goal is to leverage Federal funds by attracting substantial private and other non-Federal co-investment in critical improvements to the nation's surface transportation system."[71] TIFIA assistance may cover up to 33 percent of total eligible project costs.

Interest rates on TIFIA loans are low compared with what many private borrowers could obtain in the capital markets, and often comparable to U.S. Treasury rates. SAFETEA-LU made TIFIA loans more appealing for PPPs by lowering the project-size threshold from $100 million to $50 million, authorizing the refinancing of long-term project debt, and expanding eligible project types.[72]

The TIFIA program has been popular and appears to be successful at attracting capital. The National Surface Transportation Infrastructure

Financing Commission reports that "as of December 2008, a total of $4.8 billion of TIFIA assistance was committed to fifteen projects, facilitating over $18 billion of capital investment at a credit-subsidy cost of just $345 million."[73] The commission recommends that the TIFIA program be enhanced through increased flexibility, broadened scope, and a larger volume of credit capacity, which would encourage even greater private participation.

State Infrastructure Banks (SIBs). State Infrastructure Banks are lending organizations that consist of revolving funds—that is, loans that are continuously replenished as they are paid off. These organizations are initially capitalized with federal grants and/or state funds but are operated at the state rather than the federal level.

The SIB approach offers several advantages. First, funds can be loaned on a low-interest basis using SIBs, which helps attract private capital to a project. The loans can be secured with revenues from specific transportation projects, using flexible repayment terms. Second, SIBs are designed to complement the traditional federal-aid highway program by helping to support projects that have dedicated revenue streams. TIFIA loans focus on large projects of national or regional significance, which may leave smaller but highly valuable transportation projects without funding. The SIB approach provides states with the added flexibility to support such projects. As of December 2008, thirty-three states and Puerto Rico had established SIB programs. Although some utilized the tax-exempt bond market rather than federal funds to capitalize their SIBs, over $6 billion in loan commitments covering 609 loan agreements had been made at that time.[74]

Conclusion

This chapter and the previous one describing the benefits of PPPs are not exhaustive. Several additional benefits that I leave for future examination include the following:

- *Tax revenue accruing due to private facility provision unavailable under traditional procurement, such as corporate and property taxes.* This allows citizens to benefit directly from the enhanced value a PPP creates. Tax payments provided by the Dulles Greenway provide a case in point.

- *Avoidance through private financing of distortions (or "deadweight losses") generated by taxation that may be necessary under traditional procurement.* Empirical studies indicate that the deadweight loss from taxation in the United States is about 15 percent of total tax revenue.[75] This social loss is avoided when PPPs allow projects to proceed that would otherwise require taxation.

- *Avoidance of "project creep," or the tendency under traditional procurement for the project's focus to expand over time.* The PPP approach forces public sponsors to define the project precisely in advance and creates a contractual requirement to adhere to that plan.[76]

- *Improved accounting techniques, such as more accurate use of depreciation to account for the impact of regular use, weather, age, and so forth on a transportation facility.* One recurring problem under the traditional approach is facility deterioration, or the tendency to defer maintenance, particularly in tight budgetary periods. Accurate use of depreciation allows citizen-owners to compare that accounting number to facility maintenance and renovation. This allows quick assessment of whether the facility is being properly maintained or is being allowed to deteriorate over time.

PPPs create new opportunities for private investors relative to a government bond–only approach. Private investment introduces new, large pools of both equity and debt capital that will help revitalize U.S. transportation infrastructure. It also allows risks to be transferred to private partners, who may be better able to manage those risks. The incentives associated with private investment also have the potential to rationalize transportation investment, avoiding "white elephants" and revealing projects in which user fees can cover project costs. This exposes those parts of the system that require subsidies to operate and those that do not.

A number of policies can be pursued to attract and retain private investment in infrastructure. Given the long-lived nature of such investment, however, the most important may be the creation of a policy and regulatory environment that is stable and predictable. This reduces uncertainty, allows investors to plan for the long term, and complements America's tradition of contractual enforcement. Over time, the United States could become the premier location for global infrastructure investment.

6

The Benefits of Brownfield Public-Private Partnerships

To recap, a brownfield PPP refers to the leasing of an existing transportation facility—usually tolled—to a consortium of private firms. Although the lease typically allows the private partner to collect toll revenue in exchange for the duty to operate, renovate, maintain, and expand the facility, it is possible for a brownfield to be based on shadow tolls or availability payments.

The distinction between brownfield and greenfield PPPs may seem stark at first. However, further reflection reveals that it is actually somewhat nebulous. First, any greenfield PPP that contains a long-term operational feature has a brownfield-style PPP embedded in it. As the descriptions of PPP contractual agreements in chapter 2 suggest, a greenfield PPP can be broken down into several segments. Broad categories include the design, construction, operation, maintenance, and future expansion and refurbishment of a transportation facility. One can then imagine two different private partners: A, who contracts to complete the first two activities, and B, who contracts to undertake the last four. At some point in this process, A must hand off the operation of a completed transportation facility to B under a long-term leasing arrangement. B thus takes over the operation and maintenance of an existing facility for a specified period of time according to detailed performance specifications, which is nothing more than a brownfield concession. A greenfield concession typically bundles those two components together, which is sensible if the firm that designed and constructed the facility is also better at operating and maintaining it.

Not only is a greenfield PPP similar to a brownfield, but the reverse is also true. In a brownfield, the concessioned facility will eventually require renovation and may need complete rebuilding, especially if it is old or the lease is long. Indeed, the private partner will likely have to renovate the facility much sooner than under a greenfield PPP that delivers a new facility. The brownfield concessionaire is therefore faced with uncertain design and construction costs similar to those faced by the first partner in a greenfield case. It is also likely to confront similar labor and environmental issues, particularly if the facility is to be expanded substantially as well as renovated.

Moreover, public partners may unexpectedly have to regard a new facility as though it were a brownfield due to the risk inherent in transportation projects. If a greenfield facility is completed, but predicted traffic volume fails to materialize or other financial problems are encountered, the private partner may go bankrupt, with the facility reverting to public operation. The government is then faced with the choice of operating and maintaining the facility itself or refranchising those operations to a new partner. This is what happened with the Camino Columbia Toll Road around Laredo, Texas, as discussed in chapter 5. If it decides to accept new bids, the refranchise contract is effectively a brownfield PPP.

Commentators occasionally point to traffic or revenue risk as an important distinction between the two types of PPPs, noting that traffic flows on an existing facility are known, while they must be forecast for a new facility. Even that distinction becomes blurred with the passage of time, however, as traffic flows can change dramatically during the lease term. Traffic will be affected by economic fluctuations, expansions and contractions of nearby population centers, and the construction of competing facilities, among many other forces. Such events are difficult to predict *ex ante*. Moreover, concessionaires bidding for the lease of an existing facility will take reduced traffic risk into account. All else equal, they will bid more for the operation of a facility where there is a lesser risk of decreasing traffic, effectively transferring the market value of that lower risk to the facility's citizen-owners through the concession payment.

Two of the four U.S. brownfield concessions completed so far, the Chicago Skyway and the Indiana Toll Road, were discussed in chapter 2. Those brownfields are credited with igniting interest in PPPs in the United States, at least partly because they revealed the enormous latent value in U.S. transportation assets.[1] Public officials in each case announced a preset concession length, determined the desired details of service quality and the nature of toll regulation, and then solicited bids based on the size of the concession fee. They ensured accountability, service quality, and transparency through the concession agreement by specifying in detail how the facility was to be maintained, operated, and expanded, as well as penalties for noncompliance. The concession agreements protect the public interest in other ways. The lease could, for example, in each case be discontinued if the private partner failed to carry out its terms.[2]

Because they rely on a stream of revenue, brownfield leases are most appropriate for existing toll roads, most of which are in the eastern United States. They are therefore likely to play a secondary role to greenfield PPPs as more new facilities are built, HOT lanes are added, and so on using the PPP approach. Nevertheless, it is important that brownfield concessions be properly understood, since perceptions of them may affect both policy toward and public acceptance of PPPs generally. Indeed, many important benefits of brownfield PPPs have been underappreciated or overlooked entirely in the current policy debate. Below I provide a review of the benefits of PPPs generally that also accrue from brownfields, which also serves as a summary of some of the advantages of the PPP approach discussed in the previous two chapters.

PPP Benefits Created by Brownfield Concessions

Many of the social benefits of PPPs discussed in the previous two chapters also apply to brownfield leases. Importantly, none of the benefits summarized below depends on how concession payment proceeds are used or, indeed, on the existence of any concession payment. Stated simply, the advantages derived from private participation once a facility is complete are also generated by a brownfield concession. Those benefits include, but are not limited to, the following:

- *Injection of competition into facility operation and maintenance.* Currently, managers of existing facilities in the United States face little competition from other management teams—that is, they have a de facto monopoly over the provision of transportation-management services. They consequently need not fear replacement for poor managerial performance. A brownfield PPP also introduces the benefits of competition for the market. I discuss evidence in the next chapter documenting the savings from private involvement in facility maintenance and rehabilitation.

- *Improved lifecycle facility management (or lifecycle costing).* The brownfield concessionaire is not subject to government budget cycles that may result in deferred maintenance. Private providers have incentives to avoid costly future repairs by maintaining the asset today. They are also contractually required to do so.

- *Improved public control over the facility.* The contracting approach makes standards for maintenance, operation, and expansion transparent and enforceable. The public ultimately has better asset control.

- *Risk transfer to private partners.* As in a greenfield PPP, brownfield concessionaires face important risks even though the facility is built. Some of those risks may be better managed by private partners. Transferring risk to private partners lowers the overall cost of risk assumption.

- *Incentives to maximize traffic throughput.* Because they are affected financially, brownfield concessionaires have incentives to complete repairs quickly and with minimal disruption to traffic. Techniques to smooth flow, such as congestion pricing, will be adopted as allowed by contract. Flow maximization includes incentives to keep the roadway clear of snow and ice and well drained, which also enhances safety. The effect of all such actions is to use existing road capacity most efficiently. As noted earlier, safety on the Indiana Toll Road was enhanced after operations were taken over by the Indiana Toll Road Concession Company, which quickly worked to prevent motorists from making illegal U-turns using emergency vehicle crossovers.

- *The introduction of fresh capital.* As with constructing a new facility, the availability of capital is critical for the maintenance and renovation of an existing one. By tapping equity investors, brownfields make additional capital available.

- *The creation of new investment opportunities.* Brownfield PPPs offer distinct risk-reward profiles relative to stocks and bonds and to other investments. This creates new investment opportunities for institutional investors, such as retired police, firemen, and teachers, among others, through public pension funds.

- *The development of a "thicker" toll-operating industry.* Additional brownfield PPPs facilitate the development of the toll-operating industry, which increases the competitiveness of future PPPs. It is unsurprising that toll operators often come from countries with the greatest PPP use.[3]

- *Improvements in governance, transparency, and accounting standards.* Private participation introduces a host of mechanisms that give firm owners better control and so helps to reduce agency costs. This is a key aspect of firm governance. Private firms are also subject to rigorous accounting and reporting requirements, which improve both governance and transparency.

- *Incentives to adopt new technologies.* This is consistent with experience on brownfields. For example, the Indiana Toll Road Concession Company moved quickly to install and promote electronic toll collection in the form of its i-Zoom program.

To elaborate on the first point, bidding for brownfield leases has typically taken place on the basis of concession fee size, given fixed caps on toll increases and other dimensions of service as determined by the public sponsor. Under this approach, higher anticipated excess profits (that is, the profits above those a firm would earn in a competitive market) lead bidders to offer larger concession fees. All excess profits are transferred from the concessionaire to citizen-owners through the fee. Stated differently, the auction created by the bidding process allows citizens to realize all of a facility's latent value, as I discuss in more detail below. The well-recognized benefits of competition, which include incentives to innovate, least-cost service provision, and a customer-service orientation, can thus also be realized through a brownfield lease.

Popular literature sometimes suggests that receiving an upfront concession fee or "asset monetization" is the only motivation for private participation through a brownfield concession. As this discussion makes clear, however, a wide variety of social benefits stems from private participation in maintaining, expanding, operating, and refurbishing existing facilities that are unrelated to the payment of a concession fee. The ability to realize latent value from a facility is an important advantage, however, and I discuss it in more detail below.

Brownfield Leases Unlock Latent Value for Facility Citizen-Owners

In addition to offering the benefits mentioned above, a brownfield concession is unique in that it enhances citizen-owners' ability both to know and to capture facility value.[4] As stressed throughout, under the current approach, citizens are captive owners in the sense that they have no right to sell their ownership interest separate from their status as citizens. That makes a citizen's residual claims effectively nontransferable, unlike the claims, or shares, of every publicly traded corporation.

As a result of this nontransferability, sole government ownership and operation locks value inside a facility. Citizens are only able to realize facility value when it is either purchased by or leased to investors. Although a transportation facility may be enormously valuable, with citizens having paid for it through either tolls or taxes, their status as captive owners denies them access to that value and any reward for creating it.

The phenomenon of captive ownership is common to all state-owned enterprises. An example from another sector is illustrative. Like most transportation facilities, the U.S. Postal Service is citizen-owned. Its assets are also enormously valuable. The land and buildings American citizens own through the Postal Service alone are worth many billions of dollars.[5] Postal real estate includes substantial acreage in many prime downtown locations. One example is the James A. Farley Building in New York City, which occupies two full city blocks in downtown Manhattan and has an eight-acre footprint. The government-only ownership structure of the Postal Service, however, prevents citizens (in this case, all U.S. citizens) from realizing the latent value of such properties.

A brownfield PPP creates competition for the use of citizen-owned assets. It is uniquely beneficial because only in that way can citizens realize a facility's latent value—through the concession fee—and maintain control over it—through the concession agreement—while retaining facility ownership.

Asset-monetizing, value-extracting transactions of this sort are common in many other contexts. An initial public offering (IPO) of stock, for example, is a transaction that allows an entrepreneur or investor group to realize the value of a firm he or she may have spent years building. Similarly, a large professional partnership may go public to allow the partners to extract and enjoy the value they have created over many decades of hard work. Value extraction was one justification offered for the Goldman Sachs IPO, which represented the last major U.S. investment bank to go public.[6]

A second, related benefit is that a brownfield PPP transaction gives citizens information about the true market value of the facilities they own. Such information is useful in the case of transportation. Transportation facilities are likely to have widely differing values depending on traffic volume, competition from alternative modes and routes, pavement quality, depreciation rates, weather effects, and so on. Facilities are likely to have concomitantly varying—and challenging to determine—values. Indeed, the high values revealed by competitive bids for both the Chicago Skyway and the Indiana Toll Road concessions surprised many commentators and provided other citizen-owners throughout the country with information about the true underlying value of their own transportation facilities.

As with any asset, knowledge of value is critical in guiding decisions regarding where and how much to invest. If, for example, citizens are aware of a facility's true (high) value, they will be more willing to invest in its maintenance and expansion. Knowledge of value also provides citizens with information on the implicit rate of return they are currently receiving on their facility investment. Although information on rate of return is valuable in its own right (it can be compared to returns on other assets, for example), it also helps owners to gauge and monitor the performance of transportation facility managers; high returns—perhaps relative to some benchmark—indicate superior managerial performance, and conversely low returns, poor performance.

The capital-raising advantages of brownfields are reflected in the amounts raised, which are impressive and, as noted, often exceed expectations. The Chicago Skyway lease, for example, generated a $1.83 billion toll concession fee, but would have supported only about $800 million under traditional bond financing.[7] The concession fee paid by Brisa/CCR for Denver's Northwest Parkway raised $603 million, which is almost eighty times its annual toll revenue. This high fee partly reflects the expectation that the Denver beltway will be completed. Other U.S. brownfield leases have also brought high fees even though they were not beltway sections. Those received on the Chicago Skyway and the Indiana Toll Road were both about forty times their annual toll revenue, which is high compared to those received in other countries.[8]

Similarly, in May 2008, a group of investors led by Abertis (a Spanish toll road operator) and a Citigroup infrastructure fund offered the Commonwealth of Pennsylvania a concession fee of $12.8 billion for a seventy-five-year lease on the 537-mile tolled Pennsylvania Turnpike. That was the winning bid in a competitive process, and the largest concession fee offered to date. As a point of reference, the bid represented over one-fourth of the federal government's entire annual highway construction budget.[9] The concessionaire would also have made investments in renovation, which were badly needed, as only about 10 percent of the aging turnpike had undergone renovation as of May 2007. Also much needed were the capital improvements, in which the concessionaires would have invested $5.5 billion. Of the $12.8 billion fee, some $2.3 billion would have been used to pay off existing turnpike bonds. The net fee received by the state would then have been invested, to yield about $1.1 billion annually to fund transportation improvements throughout the state. Such a large winning bid was not anomalous or in error, as the next highest bid was close: $12.1 billion from a collaboration of Transurban and Goldman Sachs.[10] Large concession fees reflect the enormous citizen-owner value that is locked in U.S. toll facilities.

In short, brownfield leases deal with citizen-owners fairly, breaking the government's monopoly over operation of the asset and offering citizens the transaction needed to realize the latent value in the facilities they own.

Intergenerational Equity and Brownfield PPPs

For some analysts, the "intergenerational equity" effects of brownfield concessions are a matter of concern. A simple form of the argument is that brownfield leases allow current citizen-owners to extract value unfairly from future motorists, future citizens, or both. Such a concern reflects a misunderstanding of the nature of any business transaction. If the owners of a steel mill, for example, were to sell their firm to a new owner, it would be understood that the proceeds received by the current owners constituted compensation for value they had already created through their capital contributions, as well as for their managerial efforts. No one would begrudge the mill's owners the right to realize that value. Moreover, no one would suggest that the current owners were unfairly extracting value from future buyers of steel.

The price a buyer would be willing to pay is the discounted present value of the expected profit stream from the mill, which obviously would vary with anticipated revenue. This is no less true in the brownfield context, as facility value also rises or falls with projected toll revenue (that is, citizens bear the risk of changes in the market value of the facility, just like any asset owners). It is also recognized, however, that future steel customers would pay for the value they received from steel *at the time they purchased it*. Similarly, the toll paid by road customers reflects the value they receive from transportation services the facility provides at the time they use it.

A more sophisticated version of the intergenerational-equity argument is that private participants may engage in the use of excessive debt (that is, there is a risk that they will overleverage their assets) to pay large, upfront concession fees to current citizen-owners. The capital structure of the private partner, however, is of little concern to the public sponsor unless the excessive leverage is facilitated by a toll schedule that does not properly address potential market power. If tolls are regulated using a standard price-cap approach to controlling market power, and the private partner errs by taking on unserviceable amounts of debt to pay a large upfront concession fee, then current owners will simply receive more value for the lease. That risk will fall on the firm's equity and debt holders.[11] Future motorists will not pay for excessive leverage through higher tolls if the tolls are set by contract or constrained by market competition. The key insight is that, if toll rates are constrained, then the risk of over-leverage falls on investors and not on motorists or taxpayers.

That is not true if there is excessive leverage under the traditional approach, since there are no voluntary equity investors to absorb risks. Excessive leverage in the public context will manifest itself in higher borrowing costs, through either higher tolls on motorists or higher taxes on citizens, or both, rather than affecting investors who voluntarily assume that risk. The shifting of excessive debt risk onto professional investors and away from citizens must, in fact, be counted as an additional benefit of private investor participation rather than as a problem.

In sum, the intergenerational-equity argument as applied to private participation boils down to a concern about properly controlling market power. It just as readily applies to the steel mill example, where mill buyers would be willing to pay more today if they expected to be able to charge monopoly prices in the future. I address control of monopoly power in chapter 8.

The traditional approach itself creates intergenerational-equity concerns. A public-sector operator that defers maintenance and repairs due to budgetary constraints, for example, will impose a higher cost on future motorists and the taxpayers who will have to pay more to renovate the facility than if it were properly maintained over its lifecycle. By introducing proper lifecycle management, private participation ameliorates that intergenerational-equity issue.

By creating competition for the use of valuable assets, brownfield PPPs allow citizen-owners to realize the value latent in a transportation facility. The brownfield leases completed in the United States so far demonstrate that enormous value. As discussed above, brownfield leases deliver a variety of additional benefits, including improved innovation, risk transfer, lifecycle management, and better firm governance, among many others. In the following chapter, I review evidence demonstrating the benefits of greater private participation.

7

The Benefits of Private Investor Participation Demonstrated

I have already offered several illustrations of the benefits of private participation, such as completing projects on schedule, moving projects up in
time, and the cost savings of approximately 17 percent through the United
Kingdom's use of PPPs. In this chapter, I examine the record on the benefits
of private participation in greater detail. I first note evidence about the beneficial effects of private participation in a variety of countries, time periods,
and industries. This information is relevant because the benefits of PPPs in
transportation are comparable to the benefits from greater private participation in many industries and countries generally. The weight of the
evidence suggests that private participation creates large social benefits. I
then describe the use of PPPs in several countries.

Empirical Evidence on the Effects of Private Participation

The empirical literature examining the effects of privatization across time
and around the world is now massive. Its extent reflects the sweeping
nature of global privatization, which is usually dated from the large-scale
reforms in the early 1980s under the Thatcher government in Great Britain.
The ensuing wave of privatization in both developing and developed
countries resulted in a reduction in the fraction of global economic output produced by state-owned enterprises.[1] The effects of that increase in
private participation have been studied extensively, and several authoritative articles provide surveys that summarize its findings. One of the most

influential was an article by William Megginson and Jeffry Netter that appeared in the *Journal of Economic Literature* in 2001.[2]

Megginson and Netter cite 229 studies in their survey of empirical research on privatization. Using an array of data sets and statistical methods, the studies examine a wide variety of industries and many different countries and regions, including Japan, Great Britain, China, Africa, South America, Eastern and Western Europe, and the United States. They also examine different privatization methods, including asset sales, voucher (or "mass") privatizations, and share-issue privatization. They find that, overall, privatization has significantly improved firms' productivity growth, cost efficiency, and accounting performance. They also find that privatization programs have helped to modernize host countries' corporate governance systems.

Although fewer studies focus on the effects of private participation in transportation, the literature on those effects is also burgeoning. It supports the thesis that private participation improves performance, enhances efficiency, and lowers costs in a range of transportation activities. Regarding efficiency gains for taxpayers, a January 2010 study of PPPs in Canada reported that

> the second wave of Canadian P3 projects is delivering important efficiency gains for the public sector (i.e., taxpayers) relative to conventional procurement approaches. The estimated value of these gains varies from just a few million dollars per project to over $750 million in the case of the Autoroute 30 project south of the Montreal area. When these savings are expressed as a proportion of what it would have cost the public sector to procure the projects through conventional contracting methods, the savings range from 0.8 per cent through to 61.2 per cent per project.[3]

Similarly, a 2008 U.S. Department of Transportation study reported that PPPs can save 6–40 percent on construction costs and, with innovative contracting, significantly limit the potential for cost overruns.[4] A separate study of roads in France found the cost per kilometer for private road construction was 23 percent lower.[5]

In 2009, the U.S. Federal Highway Administration published a scanning study of PPPs in countries with extensive PPP experience, including Australia, Portugal, Spain, and the United Kingdom. Consistent with our foregoing discussion of the customer-service and lifecycle-management advantages of private participation, its summary of findings stated that,

> in general, the representatives of the PPP contractors the scan team met with exhibited a focus on their customers, an emphasis on life-cycle management and value, and a pride in ownership and stewardship of their assets. The comments and answers of the private participants visited demonstrated to the team members that their business model depends on these attributes.[6]

An often repeated theme in the emerging literature is that, in addition to completing projects faster, PPPs improve the *certainty* of project cost and completion times over those of traditional procurement. According to the FHWA study,

> Multiple public agencies claimed that PPP projects provide better price and time certainty on design and construction when compared to the conventional approach. Several of the countries visited indicated that the scale and complexity of and competition for PPP contracts generally lead to design and construction efficiencies, which result in better pricing and scheduling by the private sector.[7]

Commentators have noted not only that greater cost certainty is valuable in its own right, since public sponsors receive the project when they expect it, but also that it improves the allocation of public funds:

> It is important to emphasize that cost certainty in a project is not just about saving a few dollars or improving the predictability of public sector budgeting. Cost certainty is vital from a public interest perspective, because it enables public decision makers to allocate public funds to the right projects. Without cost certainty, the public sector is often compelled to allocate relatively

large amounts of additional funds midway through a project
regardless of whether the additional funding would have been
justified on a VfM basis.[8]

Private participation generates cost savings in facility operation as well
as construction. For example, a Reason Foundation analysis of U.S. toll
roads measured the "cost-take" ratio, which is the ratio of operating and
maintenance expenditures to toll revenue, for thirty-five toll facilities.[9] It
revealed that public toll authorities had a cost-take ratio of 42.6 percent,
while privately operated toll facilities averaged only 23.4 percent. In one
example, the study found that, in 2007, the Pennsylvania Turnpike spent a
surprising 62.4 percent of its toll revenues on operating and maintenance
costs. Its operating costs more than doubled between 2000 and 2007,
implying that its costs grew at 4.5 times the rate of inflation.[10]

There is also evidence on the effects of private road management and
maintenance internationally.[11] For example, in a pilot project in 1995, the
Roads and Traffic Authority in New South Wales, Australia, contracted
road maintenance to Transfield Services using a performance-based contract.[12] The authority estimated that it saved 60 percent on its maintenance
costs. Many Latin American countries, including Argentina, Brazil, Chile,
Colombia, Guatemala, and Honduras, utilized such contracts in the late
1980s and early 1990s and reported substantial savings. For example,
Brazil saved about 25 percent and Colombia 50 percent relative to public-
sector maintenance costs. Savings appear to vary between 20 and 50
percent across countries. A study of private-road associations in Sweden
also found that the cost of maintaining and operating a private road was
only half of that for an equivalent publicly managed road: about US$1.20
versus US$2.40 per meter.[13] These findings are all consistent with a broad
range of studies showing superior efficiency of private participation in an
array of industries.[14]

In the first such example in the United States, the Virginia Department
of Transportation awarded a performance-based contract for facility maintenance and operation to VMS Inc. in 1996. The contract covered 1,250
lane miles, or about 250 miles of interstate highway, and included such
aspects of maintaining and operating the highway as pavement quality,
roadside assets, bridge quality, drainage, emergency response, and snow

and ice control. VDOT estimated that it saved about 16 percent over the life of the five-and-a-half-year contract compared to what it would have spent for public-sector maintenance. That figure, however, understates the social gains from the contract that resulted from improvement in maintenance as VMS implemented a number of innovations, such as a new crack-seal program that enhanced highway pavement quality and service life.

The use of PPPs internationally in a range of economic sectors is now widespread. For example, a 2007 report on PPP use in Europe by DLA Piper includes sections on Austria, Belgium, Bulgaria, Croatia, the Czech Republic, Denmark, Finland, France, Germany, Greece, Hungary, Ireland, Italy, the Netherlands, Norway, Poland, Portugal, Romania, Scandinavia, Serbia, Slovakia, Spain, Sweden, and the United Kingdom.[15] A complete international report would include many more countries. Below I examine the transport PPP program in one country, Australia, in detail. I then briefly examine programs in France, Japan, Italy, Spain, Portugal, and the United Kingdom.

Performance of Transportation Public-Private Partnerships Abroad

The purpose of this section is to provide a flavor for the geographic and contractual diversity of transportation PPPs globally. Private facilities now operate throughout Europe, South America, and Asia. Various types of privatization of large state toll authorities have occurred in Canada, France, Italy, Japan, Portugal, and Spain, among many other countries. A few statistics illustrate the scope of those reforms. As of 2002, there were approximately 291 privately developed road projects globally, accounting for about $132 billion of project cost. The variation in project cost is huge. Smaller projects include the North Kelang Straits Urban Bypass in Malaysia, which cost $7.4 million. At the other extreme, Italy maintains the world's largest privately owned system, under which Autostrade S.p.A operates 1,950 miles of roads, including twenty toll motorways.[16] I first discuss Australia's use of transportation PPPs.

Australia. Three states in Australia—New South Wales (NSW), Queensland, and Victoria—have made extensive use of the standard greenfield

PPP model, under which private investors construct roads in return for toll revenue.[17] Until the early 1990s, most of Australia's public infrastructure was financed with current tax revenue or government borrowing. Over the subsequent fifteen years, budget pressures, combined with large, increasingly complex infrastructure projects, impelled Australia to turn to the private sector for the design, financing, construction, and management of transportation projects. By 2005, all territorial and state governments, as well as the commonwealth government, had embraced the PPP concept. A 2005 study lists more than ninety Australian PPP projects across a range of activities, either under construction, completed, or proposed.[18]

In Sydney, some noteworthy PPP projects include the Sydney Harbour Tunnel, the Hills M2 Motorway, and the Cross City Tunnel. In Melbourne, CityLink is particularly important. I briefly discuss each project in turn.

The Sydney Harbour Tunnel. Most PPPs in NSW have been used in and around Sydney. NSW's first PPP, and the one generally credited with initiating PPP use in Australia, is the Sydney Harbour Tunnel. It resulted from an unsolicited proposal in 1985 from a partnership of two companies that construct and operate transportation facilities, Transfield and Kumagai. Since the proposal was unsolicited, it was not subject to either competitive tendering or a market test—both of which are now required in Australia. The project was also unusual in that it was governed by its own legislation, which is the Sydney Harbour Tunnel (Private Joint Venture) Act of 1987. Such an act was necessary because the NSW government did not have a PPP policy apparatus in place at that time.

The state agreed that a tunnel was the best approach to addressing the heavy congestion that had developed on the Sydney Harbour Bridge in the mid-1980s, constraining the amount of traffic that could flow between North Sydney and the central business district. The NSW government, however, did not have sufficient resources to finance such a large and complex project.

Construction on the tunnel, which is 1.4 miles long and features two lanes in each direction, began in 1987. Built under a build-own-operate-transfer agreement with the NSW government, it went into service in 1992 and cost $749 million to complete. The contract length was thirty-five years, five of which were spent in construction. At the end of the operating period, in 2022, the tunnel will become an asset of the NSW government. It is noteworthy that the BOOT arrangement implies that title to the facility rests with the private partner. Actual asset ownership was important for the private partner, as it enabled it to claim depreciation for tax purposes as well as more secure collateral for financing.

Unlike in subsequent Australian transportation PPPs, the government of NSW assumed traffic risk by guaranteeing a specified minimum revenue. The NSW Roads and Traffic Authority thus made periodic, predefined payments to the private partner. It also assumed certain financing and default risks. The main risk assumed by the private partner was construction risk, which was important since geotechnical problems arose during tunnel construction. Some analysts believe that this allocation of risk was driven by the financial market's inexperience with, and thus apprehension about, PPPs in these early stages.[19]

Similarly, the private parties in this case were contractors who did not have the balance-sheet capacity of large banks, nor access to other types of equity. The Sydney Harbour Tunnel was consequently entirely debt funded, so investors were naturally more averse to revenue risk than equity investors who might have been willing to absorb it in return for higher potential returns. Without the participation of equity holders to fill this critical role, traffic risk had to be assumed entirely by the government.

The Sydney Harbour Tunnel PPP was also important because it inspired NSW to develop new policies and procedures governing the use of private participation in transportation infrastructure. Many experts believe that the development of those policies and procedures were themselves helpful in facilitating Australia's PPP activity.

The Hills M2 Motorway. Another important PPP in NSW is the Hills M2 Motorway. The Hills M2 is a twenty-one-kilometer motorway that connects the lower north shore of Sydney with Sydney's northwest regions and includes electronic express lanes to improve traffic flows. It opened to traffic in May 1997 and is now a critical part of Sydney's beltway road network, providing a link between the Lane Cove Tunnel and Westlink M7. The Hills M2 is now owned and managed by Transurban, which acquired it in 2005. Transurban has a concession to operate the M2 until 2042, after which ownership transfers to the government at no cost.

The M2 is of interest from a policy perspective. It is a real-toll BOOT PPP, implying that the private partner bears traffic risk. Unlike in the Sydney Harbour Tunnel project, the public partner makes no direct payments or guarantees to the private partner. After an examination of project risk, the auditor-general of NSW concluded, "The M2 contractual arrangements had soundly transferred and valued the project's risk," adding that "the M2 contract and financial structure was used as a model for the CityLink project in Melbourne, Australia's first fully electronic toll road."[20] Instead of receiving payments, the private operator is required to pay "land rents" to the public sector for the right to levy a toll. This is not a payment for leasing the land, but is instead actually a charge for the right to levy tolls. The payment is, however, contingent on the concessionaire's earning a predefined minimum rate of return.[21]

The Cross City Tunnel. The Cross City Tunnel (CCT) is probably Sydney's most contentious PPP. Running east to west, the 2.1-kilometer CCT links Darling Harbour to Sydney's central business district. It bypasses sixteen sets of traffic lights westbound and eighteen eastbound, reducing travel time by twenty minutes.

The concept behind the tunnel was to reduce surface traffic by encouraging it to bypass the central business district. It was hoped this would make the area more conducive to the use of public transport, cycling, and pedestrian traffic. In 2002, Cross City Motorway (CCM) Pty Ltd was awarded a DBFO contract to design, build, finance, and operate a tunnel under Sydney's central business district. The contract offered CCM no assistance from the NSW government if traffic volume failed to materialize. The concessionaire would also bear both design and construction risks.

One innovation in the CCT contract award process was the manner in which the winning contractor was chosen. In a competitive process, contractors were asked to bid on the basis of the size of a "business consideration fee" (BCF) payable to the NSW government. As on the M2 Motorway, the business consideration fee was to be paid to the government for the right to levy tolls. CCM was chosen because it offered the highest upfront payment. Of that $96.8 million, $46.1 million was a BCF component, and the remainder went to reimburse the NSW Roads and Traffic Authority for its costs related to the project.[22] This was consistent with one key goal of the project, which was to build the tunnel at no net cost to the government.

The tunnel was officially opened on August 28, 2005. Early usage was less than expected after surface streets that had been closed after the tunnel opened were reopened in response to public pressure. Surface-street closures were always part of the overall PPP plan, and indeed alleviation of surface-street congestion was in fact one of the main motivations for building the tunnel. This was, however, poorly understood by the public, which viewed surface-street closures as a way of funneling traffic off free streets and into the tolled tunnel. In November 2006, the CCT was reported to be in financial difficulty, and in December, Cross City Motorway was placed in receivership. On June 20, 2007, Leighton Contractors and investment bank ABN AMRO were designated as preferred purchasers of the Cross City Tunnel Group, which purchased the tunnel for $700 million in what was effectively a brownfield PPP.

CityLink. CityLink is a north-south set of roads that provides connections among Melbourne's airport, its ports, and its central business district by linking three existing freeways in Melbourne (Monash, Tullamarine, and West Gate). One of the system's two distinct sections, the Western Link, connects the Tullamarine Freeway to the West Gate Freeway, while the Southern Link connects the West Gate Freeway to the Monash Freeway. It is 14 miles (22 kilometers) long and, with no toll plazas, toll booths, or coin chutes, is notable for being Australia's first fully automated tollway. A cap of AUD$6.30 (about U.S.$6.13 in October 2010) on overall trip cost ensures that no matter how much of the CityLink system a motorist uses in a single trip, the total cost will not exceed AUS$6.30.

CityLink was designed and constructed under a BOOT contract in a joint venture between Transfield and the Japanese Obayashi Corporation, under contract to Transurban, at a cost of $2.2 billion. It was financed with $510 million in equity and $1.3 billion of debt and is 100 percent owned and operated by Transurban, with the concessionaire responsible for arranging financing and construction and for operating and maintaining the road. At the end of the thirty-five-year concession period, in January 2034, CityLink is to be transferred to the government. Some experts suggest, however, that the government is likely to rebid the concession in a brownfield PPP rather than absorb the ongoing costs of maintenance and expansion.

Construction of CityLink began in 1996, and the road was opened to traffic in August 1999. Despite difficulties encountered during its building, which required major tunneling and significant elevated construction, the project has been an overall financial and political success. It improves mobility in the area and was completed at almost no cost to the taxpayer. CityLink provides a high level of public satisfaction that is accomplished, in part, through innovative customer service.[23]

Early in the process of developing CityLink, the State of Victoria decided that an independent authority would handle project development and, in December 1994, established the Melbourne City Link Authority. The authority evaluated submissions for completion of the project, negotiated with interested parties, acquired the necessary land, and recommended the entity that should complete the work. It was also responsible for ensuring that the project was completed in accordance with the Melbourne City Link Act of 1995. After it was disbanded in February 2002, ongoing responsibility for managing contractual relationships was vested in VicRoads, Victoria's roads authority.

An extensive literature now exists on the performance of transport PPPs in Australia. One study, entitled *Performance of PPPs and Traditional Procurement in Australia,* focused on cost overruns.[24] It compared twenty-one PPP projects with thirty-three traditional ones and found that the relative cost savings from a PPP ranged as high as 30 percent when measured from project inception. For a contracted amount of $4.9 billion worth of PPP projects, the cost overrun was statistically indistinguishable from zero. On $4.5 billion of projects procured under a traditional model, the cost overrun was a statistically significant $673 million. PPP projects were completed ahead of time, on average, while traditional projects were completed almost 24 percent behind schedule on average. The study also found that the advantages of a PPP increased with a project's complexity and size.

The Australian experience provides evidence that PPPs provide savings in terms of completion times as well as costs. Table 7-1 compares scheduled facility opening dates with the actual opening dates for the set of transport PPPs in and around Sydney. By opening ahead of schedule in every case except one, which opened on time, motorists enjoyed an extra fifty-three months of access to these projects.

TABLE 7-1

ON-TIME PERFORMANCE OF HIGHWAY PPPS
IN NEW SOUTH WALES, AUSTRALIA

Project	Opened	Scheduled opening	Time saved
M4	May 1992	Feb. 1993	9 months
M5	Aug. 1992	Feb. 1994	18 months
Sydney Harbour Tunnel	Aug. 1992	Aug. 1992	On time
M2	May 1997	Nov. 1997	6 months
Eastern Distributor	Dec. 1999	Aug. 2000	8 months
Cross City Tunnel	Aug. 2005	Oct. 2005	2 months
Westlink M7	Dec. 2005	Aug. 2006	8 months
Lane Cove Tunnel	Mar. 2007	May 2007	2 months
Total time saved			**53 months**

SOURCE: U.S. Department of Transportation, Federal Highway Administration, *Public-Private Partnerships for Highway Infrastructure: Capitalizing on International Experience*, 2009, 47, table 10, http://international. fhwa.dot.gov/pubs/pl09010/pl09010.pdf (accessed September 1, 2009).
NOTE: Sydney is the major metropolitan area in New South Wales.

Interviews with public-sector transportation PPP experts in Australia indicate that PPPs are widely viewed as successful.[25] The key benefits stemming from PPP use there include enhanced value for money for the public sector, greater innovation in complex project settings, risk transfer, and the ability to complete projects that would be delayed for years or decades under traditional procurement. Summarizing the overall impact of the PPP initiative in Sydney, Bob Carr, former Labour Premier of New South Wales, wrote that

a business traveler from Sydney's northern suburbs can now reach the airport without a single set of traffic lights. Ten years ago the journey would have been a frustrating stop-start, high-polluting trip taking quadruple the time it now takes. A motorist can now drive all the way from northern Sydney to Canberra, even the Victorian border, without a single set of traffic lights (comparable to the journey from Washington, DC to Cleveland, Ohio)....

But here's the remarkable feature: the six major motorway projects opened in Sydney since 1995—that is, under my government—represented a total capital value of AUD$5.4 billion in new infrastructure. Of that grand total, AUD$4.6 billion came from the private sector. The capital cost to government was only AUD$800 million.[26]

The evidence from Australia's experience with PPPs in transportation is supportive of the view that substantial social benefits have been created.

France. France has a long history, going back to the *Ancien Régime*, of relying on public-private cooperation to construct infrastructure.[27] One of the first examples of a French public-private partnership is the Canal du Midi in Southern France, which was officially opened on May 15, 1681. In the nineteenth century, the French government cooperated with private firms to construct electricity, transit, railroad, sanitation, and water projects. PPPs were used in the twentieth century to build motorways and wastewater treatment plants.

The concession model was thus developed very early in France. It was accomplished under an operating form called *affermage*, whereby responsibilities for public services are transferred to a private company that is paid from fees for road use, but the projects themselves always remain under public contractual control, much like the PPP projects that have been completed in the United States.

The French model has evolved over time, and an array of projects requiring large amounts of capital are funded through what is now called *contrats de partenariat* (partnership contracts). One milestone in the development of French PPPs was a June 2004 ordinance (the *Ordonnance sur les contrats de partenariat*), which laid out the legal framework for PPPs. The institutional clarity provided by this ordinance paved the way for even greater use of PPPs. According to a January 2008 review by the Department of Economy, Finance, and Employment, the value of all French PPP contracts then in the development phase was €10 billion (about $14.7 billion at that time). Of 135 projects identified as potentially financeable via a PPP, 27 had been signed. Matthieu Desiderio reports that concession contracts helped to build and finance 75 percent of the 10,000-kilometer French motorway system.[28] PPPs have also been used to finance French high-speed passenger rail projects and light rail projects. Desiderio states, however, that while "French experience in PPP contracts is quite large… the most successful part is probably the concession/*affermage* model, to design, build, finance, operate, and maintain a network of user-financed roads and highways."[29] This is a model from which the United States can learn.

Japan. Prior to its reform in 2005, Japan's major toll authority was the world's largest, with about 4,450 miles of toll roads. The Japan Highway Public Corporation operated the system. It collected $20 billion per year in toll revenue, or about three times the amount collected by all U.S. toll authorities combined. Two much smaller toll authorities operated facilities around the main population centers of Tokyo (176 miles, operated by the Metropolitan Expressway Public Corporation) and Osaka/Kyoto/Kobe (145 miles, operated by the Hanshin Expressway Public Corporation). A fourth, the Honshu-Shikoku Bridge Authority, financed and operated about 107 miles of bridge and highway networks between Honshu and Shikoku.

On October 1, 2005, these four toll authorities were dissolved and replaced with six toll road stock companies, subject to the usual accounting and financial standards and reporting requirements. Legal title remained with a new quasi-public corporation called the Japan Expressway Holding and Debt Repayment Organization (JEHDRO). JEHDRO assumed the substantial debts of the four toll authorities and will receive lease payments from the new entities that will eventually retire those debts. This reform is perhaps best understood as "corporatization," or an organizational change that is a step toward privatization, since the government continues to hold all the stock in the new entities. Further steps toward private participation appear to be entangled in political wrangling.[30]

Spain. Spain also has a history of privately owned toll roads going back to the 1960s, although legislation dating from 1953 allowed private firms to construct toll roads for a maximum term of seventy-five years.[31] Several concessions were granted to begin development in 1964 of the National Expressway System, which envisaged the construction of about 1,864 miles of expressways in Spain by 1980. Specific legislation was passed for each concession as a way to speed construction. Concessionaires were, in some cases, granted very favorable terms.

In 2003, the Spanish state toll agency, ENA Infraestructuras SA, which included five toll roads accounting for 288 miles of road, was acquired for $1.8 billion by Sacyr-Vallehermoso in competitive bidding. That group accounts for about 16 percent of the total number of Spanish toll roads. Sacyr-Vallehermoso and Abertis jointly control Avasa, which accounts for about 10 percent of the total mileage. Although Spain's toll road companies faced financial challenges in the 1970s, they have been very profitable since the early 1990s and have expanded their presence in Latin America and in new markets in Europe.[32]

Spain uses a combination of real and shadow tolls.[33] Importantly, the lack of sufficient revenue from real tolls does not preclude the use of a PPP in Spain. The government determines if traffic volume will permit real toll use. If not, shadow tolls are utilized.[34] About 88 percent of the National Highway System mileage under a PPP contract uses real tolls, while almost 12 percent relies on shadow tolling.

In its international study, the Federal Highway Administration noted the importance of PPPs in constructing Spain's National Highway System:

> Similar to Portugal, Spain has built a majority of its National Highway System through concessions and, in the near future, will have more than half of this system under active PPP concessions. Since the 1960s, Spain has pioneered the concession model for infrastructure development and has continuously sought better ways to improve the effectiveness and efficiency of its approach. Along the way, it has built a global industry that is positioned to provide highway development, operations, and financial services anywhere in the world.[35]

Portugal. The original, and largest, toll road operator in Portugal is Brisa. Brisa was a private company when it was granted a tolled motorway concession in 1972. The Portuguese government took a majority stake in Brisa in 1974 following the Carnation Revolution.[36] It remained a state-owned enterprise until the 1990s, when it was privatized in stages. Its privatization raised about $2 billion. One of the government's key motivations for privatizing Brisa was to promote competition in the industry.[37] Brisa, which is now one of the largest companies traded on the Lisbon stock exchange, operates eleven toll roads totaling over 621 miles and was a pioneer in the development of electronic tolling. Five other firms operate the remaining toll roads in Portugal.

Portugal administers PPPs in an innovative way. A state-owned enterprise called Estradas de Portugal SA (EP) was created in 2005 to oversee the development of Portugal's national highway network. EP executes future PPP agreements under a seventy-five-year concession agreement with the Portuguese government.

In 2004, Finance Minister Antonio Mexia announced that Portugal would impose tolls on all its motorways, stating that free roads "are no longer financially viable."[38] At the time, about two-thirds of the country's motorways were toll roads, and about one-third were not. Both real and shadow tolls are now used to support Portuguese PPPs. Real tolls are typically used when traffic volume exceeds 15,000 vehicles daily, while shadow tolls are used below 10,000 vehicles. Of the 1,553 miles of roads under PPP contracts, about 53 percent are subject to real tolls, while 37 percent are shadow-tolled,[39] and about 8 percent are untolled. Also in use are innovative hybrids of shadow tolls, real tolls, and availability payments, the mixture of which is dependent on traffic volumes. Portugal is considering eliminating shadow tolls on roads that generate sufficient revenue from real tolls.[40]

Future use of PPPs is largely determined by Portugal's National Road Plan. The plan, the country's framework for highway development, was last updated in 2000. Portugal expects to rely mostly on PPPs to complete its National Motorway System.[41]

United Kingdom. The United Kingdom has also used transportation public-private partnerships extensively.[42] Indeed, some view Britain as the world leader in PPP use. The first design-build highway contract was awarded in 1990, and the Private Finance Initiative (PFI) of 1992 expedited private participation. Notably, the PFI was "intended to facilitate closer co-operation between the public and private sectors and introduce private sector skills and disciplines into the delivery and management of projects and services traditionally undertaken by the public sector."[43] Prior to that initiative, the Highways Agency—the United Kingdom's main governmental entity responsible for roads, bridges, and tunnels— relied on a traditional approach using primarily public funding sources to construct and maintain major motorways.

In August 1994, the Highways Agency announced that eight motorway and trunk road projects would be delivered through PPPs using design-build-finance-operate contracts. Those early projects were almost completely financed using shadow tolls because of resistance to real tolls.

Given the endemic U.S. problem of excessively long project delivery times, Britain's "early contractor involvement" approach is noteworthy. Under it, the contractor is engaged in the process very early, often in the planning stage, and that involvement continues into the project completion and facility management stages. The Highways Agency estimates that project delivery times have fallen significantly as a result, from an average of eleven years to five years.

Other goals of the British PPP program are relevant for the United States, particularly with regard to risk transfer, innovation, and the development of a domestic facility-operating industry. For example, the Highways Agency states that

> the Agency formally launched its use of PFI to procure a road service on parts of the motorway and trunk road network in August 1994. The Agency's objectives for each DBFO project were:
>
> - to ensure that the project road is designed, maintained and operated safely and satisfactorily so as to minimise any adverse impact on the environment and maximise benefit to road users;
>
> - to transfer the appropriate level of risk to the private sector;

- to promote innovation, not only in technical and operational matters, but also in financial and commercial arrangements;

- to foster the development of a private sector road-operating industry in the UK; and

- to minimise the financial contribution required from the public sector.[44]

Recent studies suggest that the PFI has achieved those objectives. According to a 2007 U.S. Federal Highway Administration study of the international use of PPPs,

> In the past twelve years, both public and private sectors in England have gained significant experience and confidence in using PPPs to fund and deliver infrastructure assets. According to Standard & Poors, more than £48 billion in total capital has been invested in PPP projects in England to date with up to £64 billion in additional capital investment via PFI over the next sixteen years.[45]

The United Kingdom has also developed a "programme of major schemes," as well as regional transportation plans. A variety of factors must be considered to determine the preferred project delivery method, but a private financing approach must be considered first for any major scheme, which is defined as a project exceeding £7.5 million in capital cost.[46]

The empirical evidence presented in this chapter indicates that significant social benefits have been generated by the greater private participation in highway design and construction undertaken in almost all global regions since the early 1980s. The evidence suggests that private involvement in road management and operation has also generated benefits for society overall. To capture all the benefits of PPPs, however, consideration of several important policy issues by prospective public partners prior to entering into contracts with private partners is critical, as I discuss in the next chapter.

8

Public-Private Partnerships
in the Public Interest

As we have seen, public-private partnerships have been used successfully in many developed and developing countries outside the United States. They are productively employed (though under different names) in a variety of similarly structured U.S. industries in which private investors provide capital crucial to the industry's growth and development. They are already generating social benefits in the U.S. transportation sector in both the greenfield and brownfield contexts.

Prospective public-sector partners should not enter into these complex agreements, however, until they have addressed several important policy issues and laid the necessary groundwork for truly successful partnerships. Successful PPPs require their own infrastructure of an institutional nature. Potential public sponsors in the United States are very well positioned to address such questions, as they can now draw on vast international experience. Other countries confronted many of these same questions long ago, and a number of studies are now available that consider carefully the protection of the public interest via the PPP agreement.[1]

Managing the PPP Process

The process of initiating, negotiating, and managing a PPP over time is complex. It generates a variety of issues that public sponsors should consider carefully, several of which I discuss here. First I address the question of developing a consensus among various affected groups regarding the PPP approach, which include motorists and taxpayers as well as members of the state legislature. I next focus on the importance of building public-sector knowledge, experience, and expertise pertaining to all aspects of PPPs. I then discuss the importance of transparency of the PPP process, innovative auction approaches, and contract enforcement.

Public-Sector Consensus. Perhaps the most basic prerequisites to successful PPP use are thorough investigation, discussion, deliberation, and ultimate agreement among public-sector stakeholders regarding the desirability of private participation. Public officials may wish to undertake a comprehensive assessment of their state's or locality's unique current and future transportation needs and finances, and to consider carefully how PPPs fit into its overall transportation system and program. While undertaking such studies and holding hearings on PPPs is one way to bring about consensus, a more affirmative approach on the state level is to pass PPP-enabling legislation. The discussion of such legislation explicitly places the PPP question on legislative and executive agendas and allows various groups to express their views, either directly in hearings or through their elected representatives. It also gives investors a measure of confidence that their efforts in developing a proposal and moving it forward will not be frustrated by disagreement among public-sector stakeholders after the fact.[2] These laws help define the institutional setting for potential investors and public-sector sponsors alike.

Building a solid consensus among public-sector participants is particularly important, as the failure of the proposed lease of the Pennsylvania Turnpike made clear. In assessing what undermined the lease, the Pew Center on the States explained that when Governor Edward G. Rendell decided to pursue the lease soon after the Pennsylvania legislature had passed a landmark transportation bill, members "were confused by the timing of the governor's decision and felt they had been excluded from the process."[3]

Careful discussion and study of PPPs by potential public sponsors, and the achievement of consensus prior to negotiations with private partners, is thus a key prerequisite for successful private participation.

Public-Sector Expertise. When PPPs are used widely in a city or state, officials need to assume new roles, performing such functions as the screening of bidders, contract negotiation, contract monitoring and enforcement, and, possibly, renegotiation. Once a consensus emerges that PPPs are desirable, public sponsors should develop an understanding of each of these issues surrounding private participation, with a focus on protecting the public interest.

Such public-sector expertise is important because public-private partnerships can be complex and are relatively new to the U.S. transportation sector. Officials can and should seek outside advice wherever necessary. Moreover, a city or state may wish to create a specialized office to interact with private participants, or at least assign that responsibility to a specific group. Some jurisdictions in other countries have created such specialized offices, charged with providing expertise and promoting private investment. Examples include Partnerships British Columbia in Canada,[4] Partnerships Victoria in Melbourne,[5] and Infrastructure Australia in Sydney.

Developing public-sector expertise helps ensure that officials obtain favorable terms for citizen-owners, which is one of their duties as citizens' agents. These include not only proper maintenance and expansion standards, but also appropriate concession fees for owners. The development of expertise also alleviates fears of unequal bargaining skills between public and private participants, thus enhancing public acceptance of PPPs in the long term.

Process Transparency. Since transparency in the PPP process increases public confidence and enhances stakeholder support, all stages should be as transparent as possible, as officials in countries with extensive PPP experience emphasize.[6] Transparency has costs as well as benefits, however, and basic economics provides one rationale for maintaining some confidentiality: competing private participants may "free ride" off the efforts other bidders invest in developing a PPP proposal. The social problem with free riding is that private parties will have less incentive to put in the hard work necessary to generate a solid, informed PPP proposal if they believe competitors will use that information to their own advantage without incurring the cost. Overall, too little private-sector effort in the PPP process will be made if free riding is allowed. Moreover, private parties may refuse to participate altogether if they are forced to reveal company secrets. As with other dimensions of PPP contracts, public officials must strive to reach the correct degree of transparency in the process, which is likely to vary depending on the details of the PPP in question.

Innovative Auction Approaches. Scholars studying the use of PPPs in transportation have suggested innovative alternatives to standard maximum-concession-fee/minimum-toll approaches to franchise auctions.[7] One approach, which focuses on concessions of the build-operate-transfer type, makes use of variability in concession length. Here the public partner predetermines the maximum acceptable toll, service quality standards, and other dimensions of the agreement, and concessionaires then bid on the basis of the lowest present value of toll revenue they will accept. The franchise comes to an end when the toll revenue received by the winning concessionaire equals the amount they bid. The concession can then be rebid or revert to public-sector operation. This type of an auction is called a least present value of revenue (LPVR) auction.

One advantage of an LPVR auction is that it ameliorates the effects of traffic (or revenue) risk on the private partner. If traffic is unexpectedly low, depressing revenues, then the franchise automatically lasts longer to ensure that investors receive their anticipated return on investment. Conversely, if traffic is unexpectedly high, the franchise period is shorter. LPVR auctions have been used successfully in Chile.[8] Their application to U.S. PPPs should be explored in more detail, perhaps through experiments.

Under any auction approach, public-sector sponsors must pay careful attention to the contracting process so that citizens realize the benefits of competition. Although lack of consensus eventually precluded it, commentators lauded the process through which Pennsylvania chose the winning bidder for its turnpike lease.[9] The state issued a request for qualifications in September 2007. Fourteen bidders initially expressed interest. The final stage of the bidding process, which generated $2 billion in additional value for citizen-owners, has been summarized as follows:

> Only four bidders, including Citi Infrastructure Investors and the Spanish firm Abertis Infraestructuras, remained during the final months of the process; those two companies ultimately merged their proposals into a single bid and competed against Goldman Sachs and Abertis/Cintra for the lease. When the two

highest bidders, Goldman Sachs and Abertis/Citi submitted bids within 10 percent of each other, the state called them back for a best and final offer round. Abertis/Citi raised additional capital from lending institutions that had been supporting Macquarie/Cintra and increased its bid by more than $2 billion in the final round.[10]

Although the use of a best and final offer would have generated added value for facility owners had the Pennsylvania contract been completed, care must be taken in the bidding process to balance those added benefits against the higher costs imposed on bidders of such an approach.

Contract Enforcement. When PPPs are used, the public sponsor has a responsibility to monitor and enforce the terms of the agreement. Public partners should carefully consider how they will ensure that contractual terms are enforced. A clearly defined public entity that will objectively assess compliance with contractual responsibilities should be given a mandate to verify that private partners are upholding service quality, maintenance standards, and other key requirements of the contract.

The design of contracts can also make them easier to enforce. Wisely designed contracts align the for-profit incentives of private partners with the public interest. For example, Autostrade, the largest concessionaire of roads in Italy, is allowed to increase tolls by more than the rate of inflation if it improves road quality by a specific amount. This compensates the operator for enhancing road quality.

Fortunately, as mentioned earlier, transportation facility operation is an activity in which contractual compliance is usually observable. Variables such as traffic throughput, facility expansion, service quality (including promptness of debris removal), and pavement quality are easily monitored, lowering the cost of contract enforcement.[11] New technologies, such as systems for monitoring concrete quality, will further reduce the cost of enforcement as they are adopted. Moreover, the costs of contract monitoring and enforcement need not affect public budgets even if they are substantial. The PPP agreement can specify that the private partner pay these costs, as is the case under both the Indiana Toll Road and Chicago Skyway concession agreements.[12]

Experience suggests that contracts should focus on performance outcomes rather than mandating specific input use. This reflects a recognition that motorists are, in fact, the facility's customers, and performance should focus on their needs. Contracts should, for example, mandate standards for road surface quality rather than for how many workers a PPP employs in road maintenance. This gives the private partner flexibility to use the best mixture of inputs to achieve a certain benchmark, which is likely to vary across climates, facilities, and providers.

Addressing Potential Market Power

One of the most critical policy issues facing potential private sponsors is that of properly addressing the market power potentially held by a private participant. The operator of a facility, whether public or private, possesses market power if there are few alternatives to a particular road, bridge, or tunnel—that is, when competition from other modes of travel and facilities is weak. If a bridge is one of only a few ways to get to a certain destination, for example, then a firm can raise tolls above those that would be forthcoming in a competitive market. This leads to an inefficiently small number of vehicles using the facility.[13] The policy goal is to create the set of institutional arrangements that achieves the best, or optimal, toll level, and thus results in the correct number of vehicles using the facility.

Although a higher toll reduces the number of vehicles (that is, customers), an operator with sufficient market power may still have an incentive to impose high tolls. Depending on the sensitivity of traffic volume to the toll (that is, on the price elasticity of demand), the additional revenue received per vehicle can more than compensate the firm for the reduced throughput. Notably, the problem with market power from an economic perspective is not that the firm's profits are "excessive," but, again, that its behavior results in too few vehicles using the facility.[14] The policy focus should, therefore, be not on the firm's rate of return, but on the actual tolls charged.

Such pricing concerns are, of course, not unique to transportation. They arise whenever there are few (or only one) providers of a critical good or service. As a result, discussion and analysis of appropriate policies to address this issue have been extensive. I offer here several insights from related experience in other industries.

Toll Regulation Is Necessary Only When Competitive Forces Are Weak. The regulation of tolls through a concession agreement is a substitute for within-market competition.[15] It is an attempt to use legal processes (here contracts rather than direct regulation) to mimic the constraining effect of competition on price. In any industry, where competition is robust, firms have little pricing power, so prices will be close to marginal cost. Under competition, firms are only able to earn a "normal" rate of return,[16] in which case price regulation is not needed, either through contracts or through a regulatory body.

Transportation facilities are likely to face more competition than many other utilities. An electric utility, for example, may possess substantial market power because it provides the only source of power into a home or business. In contrast, a particular highway may face competition both from other modes of travel and from competing routes. Consider the market power held by a hypothetical operator of Interstate 95 between Boston and New York. The market power of such an operator may seem substantial, but it is constrained by available alternatives. Motorists who wish to travel between Boston and New York may choose among flying, driving, or taking a train. Even those committed to driving may choose among several alternative routes. If, for some reason, they are even more constrained and forced to use I-95, they can still choose to carpool, take a bus, or drive during off-peak hours. All these alternatives and actions work to weaken—but not eliminate—the market power of I-95's operator.[17] One can, of course, imagine unusual transportation situations (such as a bridge to an island with no airport or ferry service) in which a facility operator might have substantial market power, but many transportation facilities are likely to face at least some competition from alternative routes and modes.

As this discussion implies, the intensity of competition, and thus market power, will vary greatly across transportation facilities. This has important implications for the stringency of price regulation, which should, if properly administered, vary inversely with the degree of competition. Given that the purpose of regulation is to mimic market competition, price regulation should be relaxed as competition rises, so the best regulatory approach will also vary over time. A one-size-fits-all approach to regulation should be avoided. Rather, regulation of market power in transportation through contracts is best determined on a case-by-case basis, after careful consideration by public sponsors, based on the available alternative modes and routes of travel.

Market Power Should Be Addressed through Incentive Regulation. Two broad approaches to controlling potential market power are rate-of-return regulation (RORR), which focuses on controlling the return earned by the regulated firm, and incentive regulation, which focuses on controlling the prices the firm charges.[18]

Economists agree that RORR has some undesirable properties.[19] Most obviously, a firm whose rate of return is fixed by regulation has little incentive to operate efficiently or assume risk, since it will receive no higher return for doing so. Its incentives to minimize costs, take risks, adopt cost-reducing innovations, and maintain a customer-service orientation are blunted.[20] It is critical that the firm, although price-regulated if necessary, retain those salutary incentives, which can only be achieved if the firm stands to capture the benefits of innovation and cost-reducing efforts.

RORR has other undesirable side effects. For example, a firm whose rate of return is based on its capital input has an incentive to overcapitalize. This is known as the Averch-Johnson effect.[21] Moreover, because RORR requires constant monitoring of the firm's costs, it is complex and costly to administer. Even with regular monitoring, the firm will always have better information on its costs than that possessed by the regulator, which makes effective RORR difficult—a problem that has been recognized in the PPP context. In comparing equity internal rate-of-return (IRR) caps—which are roughly equivalent to RORR—with revenue sharing, the Legislative Study Committee on Private Participation in Toll Projects in Texas says that

> equity IRR caps have a similar effect of reducing developer profits, but can prove more complicated in practice. Unlike revenue sharing, which is ultimately based on a single, easily verifiable, variable—revenue—the determination of equity IRRs

requires the assessment of a number of disparate factors, including
the condition of the credit markets at the time of the calculation
and the specific level of risk assumed by the project's developer.[22]

Additionally, some transportation projects may not generate profits
for many years. For example, profits are generally not realized on a greenfield project in the first ten to fifteen years of a concession agreement.[23]
For investment in such a case to be rational, profits in the later years of a
project must be sufficient to offset early losses. If a regulatory body were
to look only at rates of return in later years (and ignore early-year losses),
it might find the rate of return to be "unreasonable" and more stringent
regulation warranted. That would have the unintended, undesirable consequence of deterring future investment. More fundamentally, it is impossible
to determine a reasonable or fair rate of return a priori, since varying
anticipated rates of return may be necessary to draw capital to different
projects.[24] Some projects that carry greater risk will require a higher
return to attract capital.

For these reasons, some form of incentive regulation, in particular the
price cap, is the dominant approach to PPP regulation internationally. In
general, price-cap regulation limits the prices charged by the regulated firm,
but there are a variety of permutations. The price could simply be fixed at
a given level, which in the transportation context means that the toll in real
terms falls over time. More commonly, however, the price cap is allowed to
rise with some inflation index, such as the Consumer Price Index. Another
alternative, used in other regulatory contexts in the United Kingdom, is to
allow prices to increase at the rate of inflation, minus an adjustment factor
(sometimes interpreted as adjusting for anticipated productivity improvements), which is referred to as an X-factor.[25]

The important aspect of price-cap regulation is that the firm's incentive
to innovate, reduce costs, and focus on safety and customers is retained
while monopoly power is controlled. Commentators have recognized the
superiority of price caps over RORR. According to Grimsey and Lewis,
for example,

> In those activities which have natural monopoly characteristics,
> substitution of price-cap regulation for rate-of-return regulation

(i.e. fixing of maximum prices rather than the mark up over costs) has created strong incentives to reduce costs, while third party access to certain facilities that are not economic[al] to duplicate has widened competition in the upstream and downstream markets served by the facilities.[26]

The regulatory focus should, therefore, be on the price paid by consumers rather than on the firm's profits or rate of return at any particular time. The United States would likely benefit from more experimentation in the use of incentive regulation of transportation PPPs.

An important policy question is whether toll caps interfere with a firm's ability to implement congestion prices. The obvious problem is that tolls high enough to regulate traffic flow may violate a toll cap. One simple solution is to impose a cap on the average toll over some time period—for example, a day or a week—which allows tolls to exceed the cap within that time frame if there are compensating low tolls during off-peak times. Reflecting the demand for more investment in some areas, zero tolls may be necessary in off-peak times to compensate for the congestion prices necessary to limit demand during peak times.

For this and other reasons, commentators have recommended a revenue-sharing approach. Revenue sharing requires the concessionaire to remit a specified percentage of toll revenues (usually above some threshold) to the public sponsor. In the PPP covering segments 5 and 6 of State Highway 130 in Texas, for example, the percentage of revenue shared rises on a sliding scale as toll revenue rises, reaching fifty-fifty at a certain point.[27] The public sponsor must still monitor tolls to ensure they are not set higher than the free-flow level to extract monopoly profits, which would create a social loss.

The United States could experiment with other innovative approaches to controlling market power while preserving salutary incentives. For example, the concession contract for the 407 Express Toll Route in Canada gives the private operator, the Spanish firm Cintra, the ability to set its tolls but assesses penalties on the firm if it fails to attract adequate traffic from untolled roads that run parallel to 407.[28] This constrains the operator's ability to raise tolls to a level that would restrict traffic flows but also provides an incentive to expand the facility as necessary.

Additional Contracting Issues

Although there are many additional contracting issues, I here discuss two particularly salient questions that public sponsors may wish to consider before entering into public-private partnerships. Those are noncompete (or compensation) clauses, and the use of concession payments.

Noncompete Clauses and Compensation Clauses. Noncompete clauses in PPP contracts have been a contentious issue in the United States, in part because of the controversy in California surrounding the California 91 Express Lanes noncompete clause.[29] A noncompete clause is a pledge by the public partner that it will not build an unplanned, competing transportation facility within a specified distance of the privately operated facility.

Strict noncompete clauses appear to be rare, having been replaced by compensation clauses. Here the public partner may construct an unplanned competing facility but, using a predetermined formula, is required to compensate the private partner for revenues lost from the added competition.[30] The Indiana Toll Road concession agreement, for example, requires the state to compensate the concessionaire for lost revenues if the state constructs, within ten miles of the Indiana Toll Road, a new interstate-quality highway of twenty or more continuous miles.[31] In some countries, compensation clauses are complementary to a "compensable enhancement" clause, under which the private partner compensates the relevant public sponsor for increased revenue generated by an unplanned facility, such as a new interchange or access road.[32]

The reason for a noncompete/compensation clause is straightforward: investors, especially either government or private bondholders, will be loath to invest knowing that the government can use its unique, inalienable power of taxation to compel funding of an untolled, "free" road that will compete with the facility they expect to generate the cash flow necessary to pay back their investment. These clauses thus evolved to assure buyers of toll-revenue bonds that traffic would not be diverted from the toll road, thus reducing the ability of the concessionaire to repay debt.[33] Because competition from a "free" road will affect the holders of bonds issued by either a public or a private entity, compensation clauses have also been granted to publicly operated toll roads. Any bondholders who anticipate being paid back out of the facility's toll revenue are likely to demand guarantees against competing "free" roads.[34]

A historical example illustrates the problem that free facilities can cause for toll roads. On February 18, 1928, the U.S. Highway 11 bridge across Lake Pontchartrain in Louisiana was opened to traffic.[35] The bridge is almost five miles long and carried over 23,000 vehicles per day in 2006. It was built with private funds as a toll facility by a group of contractors called the Watson-Williams Syndicate. The populist governor Huey P. Long, who campaigned on the promise of "free" bridges, entered office soon afterward and built competing untolled bridges at the Rigolets and the Chef Menteur Pass. Unsurprisingly, the Watson-Williams Bridge suffered a severe drop in traffic and, thus, in revenues. Its owners were eventually forced to sell it to the State of Louisiana for pennies on the dollar. The effect on both equity and debt holders was ruinous.

This is not an isolated case. The U.S. Government Accountability Office blames the rise of tax-financed "free" roads, along with railroads, for the decline of private toll roads, which were prevalent in the nineteenth century.[36] Investors (whether in private debt or equity or in government debt) continue to fear ruinous competition from tax-funded alternatives, so compensation clauses are often necessary to attract capital to infrastructure projects.[37] Since compensation clauses could be perceived as enhancing a private operator's monopoly power, as well as constraining public officials, it is important that the public understand their history and the rationale behind them, and that they be fully explained before a PPP agreement is concluded. To the extent that a compensation clause, in fact, increases the firm's market power, it should be reflected in toll caps. Daniels and Trebilcock offer the following example of the interaction between toll regulation and compensation clauses, with reference to the Prince Edward Island Fixed Link in Canada, which was built by SCI:

> To safeguard SCI's franchise, the contract between the federal government and the developer limited the government's ability to compete with the project by providing ferry service or constructing an additional bridge or tunnel within 25 km of the fixed link or by any means that would significantly reduce traffic volumes. However, in light of the monopoly power conferred

on the operator by this restriction, the contract imposed limits on permissible increases in bridge tolls by the operator to 75% of CPI.[38]

Noncompete agreements also appear in the context of other utilities, albeit under different names. That is unsurprising, since investors will be hesitant to invest in any long-lived, sunk asset that may face future competition from a subsidized entity. Electric utilities, for example, have historically been granted "exclusive territories" where competition from other companies, public or private, is disallowed.

The Use of Concession and User-Fee Payments. While not directly involving the PPP contract itself, an important public-sector decision, particularly with regard to brownfield PPPs, is how to use concession proceeds properly.[39] This question also applies to funds generated by fuel taxes and vehicle miles traveled charges and arises any time the public sector receives payments that are not contractually precommitted to a certain purpose.

The basic problem is how to ensure that payments are not diverted to uneconomical projects or used to indulge the preferences of those controlling them. This is another manifestation of the agency problem,[40] and it affects private firms, state-owned enterprises, and governments generally. In corporate finance, it is known as the "agency problem of free cash flows." For a private firm, free cash flows are defined conceptually as the cash flows the firm receives from its business operations in excess of those necessary to fund all available profitable projects.[41] They are in some sense "excess," uncommitted cash flows, and they generate agency problems because they lead to increased managerial discretion over resources. Managers may use them to indulge their own preferences, such as through excessive compensation, perks, or unprofitable acquisitions. Similarly, government managers, including politicians, may use free cash flows in a wasteful way—for example, on projects that have little economic value but are helpful in securing reelection. The challenge in both cases is getting managers to disgorge free cash flows to firm owners (that is, shareholders or citizen-owners) before they are wasted. Addressing the agency problems associated with free cash flows is one aspect of good firm governance.

Private firms can disgorge free cash flows to firm owners in a number of ways, such as through one-time dividend payments or share repurchases. Because free cash flows depress share prices, private firms that persistently refuse to disgorge them to firm owners are also subject to takeovers. Indeed, this is a leading theory of takeovers.[42] State-owned enterprises, in contrast, cannot repurchase shares or be taken over. In the interest of good governance, it is therefore critical for governments to consider carefully other ways of reducing the agency costs associated with free cash flows.

Although their choices are more limited, public sponsors can take steps to reduce the agency problems associated with free cash flows. Even though a brownfield concession fee does not generate a flow of cash, public sponsors could mimic a dividend payout by directly rebating to citizens of the relevant jurisdiction the concession fee on a per-capita basis.[43] This reduces agency problems since the fee is disgorged while explicitly recognizing the citizen as facility owner. The public sponsor can also help to reduce discretion and lower agency costs by precommitting proceeds to projects that are expected to have positive net present values. One such example is the use of proceeds from leasing the Indiana Turnpike to fund the Major Moves program in that state.[44]

Sponsors can, of course, convert the concession fee into a flow of payments by investing them in a fund yielding a given rate of return. The problem then becomes reducing the agency problems associated with that cash flow. One way of reducing the discretionary use of funds is to ensure that they are used for transportation purposes only, which has the advantage of strengthening the user-pays principle. Indeed, most state-level restrictions on proceed use require that proceeds be deposited into some type of transportation trust fund.[45] Regardless of whether funds originate from fuel taxes, VMT charges, or concession fees, governments must take steps to ensure that they are used efficiently and that the agency costs of free cash flows are reduced.

Under the PPP approach, monies paid by motorists to use a facility are contractually required to be used for maintaining, operating, and expanding that facility. This reduces the risk of their being diverted to noneconomic activities, and thus lowers the agency costs associated with those cash flows. This advantage is enhanced by the financing of many infrastructure projects under a project financing model, whereby the loans required to build the facility are secured by the facility's assets and paid entirely from project cash flow.[46]

Ex Post Opportunism

Most PPP contracts are likely to be long term, and for good reason. Long-term contracts attract capital to a project that might otherwise go unfunded. They encourage a long-term horizon so that investors are willing to absorb losses in early years, secure in the knowledge that their investment will be recouped later. Like all contracts, PPP contracts are incomplete. This simply means that the contract does not address how the risk of all possible contingencies will be dealt with. Incompleteness arises because it is costly to describe in a contract all the contingencies that might arise and to specify how those risks are to be apportioned. The problems associated with contract incompleteness obviously worsen with the contract term.

The main policy problem stemming from contract incompleteness in the long term is *ex post* opportunism, also called a holdup problem. Holdup problems occur when one contracting party attempts to use the leverage stemming from its unique position to extract better terms from the other party. In this case, the unique position stems from the fact that transportation assets are sunk and are specific to the parties in question, so one or both parties may engage in *ex post* opportunism should a contingency arise that is not discussed in the contract.

Holdup problems are also likely to be heightened in transportation infrastructure because one contracting party is a government entity. The government has certain inalienable legislative powers, and legislatures face challenges in precommitting to future policies—that is, because public partners by law cannot forswear their power to tax and regulate, a private investor assumes the risk that the value of a PPP lease, for example, will decline due to some government action.[47] Actions may take the form of, among others, building competing "free" facilities, as noted above, or of imposing regulation in the future that excessively depresses toll rates and, thus, the value of the lease. Even in highly developed countries such as Canada, the strength of governmental contractual commitments is in question because the legislature can abrogate contracts. This may have a chilling effect on private investment.

The existence of holdup problems in such industries has sparked a debate in the economics profession on the viability of franchise bidding over the long term and whether it will devolve into ongoing regulation.[48] Importantly, the decision about including private partners in transportation funding does not turn on the outcome of this debate. Substantial, successful, long-term investor funding takes place even in industries where holdup problems loom large, such as electricity and ports.

More directly, holdup problems suggest a need to keep contracts flexible and maintain solid, ongoing relationships between contracting parties. The contract can then be modified as necessary to ensure that the relationship remains beneficial to both. Such modifications occur in Spain, for example, where renegotiation is referred to as "rebalancing" the concession agreement. Rebalancing was also done for the Dulles Greenway concession when the original concession term of forty years was renegotiated to sixty years.[49] The concession deed that governs CityLink in Melbourne has been amended twenty-nine times.[50] Referring to practices across countries, the Federal Highway Administration informs us that

> *practices for managing changes and uncertainty throughout the contract period vary and range from rebalancing actions to limited material adverse effect impacts.* Rebalancing is a significant modification process, but one that is intended to be applied symmetrically. The conditions can be modified in either the public or private sector's favor (emphasis in original).[51]

Rebalancing can occur both to protect the public interest and to retain investment. The public partner may, for example, wish to extend the concession length if expected traffic flows do not materialize to allow the private partner to recoup its investment. Experience also suggests that it is better to address contracting concerns as they arise rather than allow them to accumulate into a major renegotiation.[52] Indeed, the ability to address such concerns and maintain an ongoing relationship speaks to the essential meaning of a public-private partnership.

International experience suggests that public and private partners can effectively address such contracting problems over the long term. The Federal Highway Administration study reported on second- and sometimes third-generation PPPs.[53] Although many of the concessions examined are in the thirty- to forty-year range, successful concessions in France and other countries can run as long as seventy years.[54] Clearly, therefore, despite contracting problems associated with asset specificity, PPPs are viable over the long term.

Overall, PPPs generate a number of public policy concerns that must be considered carefully prior to entering into an agreement. In countries with limited experience in using transportation PPPs, such as the United States, a change in public-sector focus and an enhancement in expertise is called for. Public sponsors need to contract effectively with private participants, which includes addressing such questions as building a public consensus, franchise bidding, contract monitoring and enforcement, potential market power, and the use of concession payments, among many others. I have addressed only a few here. The analysis in the previous chapters, however, suggests that the benefits of introducing private participation are worth the effort.

Summary and Conclusions

The traditional approach to financing, operating, and maintaining transportation infrastructure served America well for decades. The Interstate Highway System, many rural and urban roads, and numerous bridges and tunnels were successfully built and maintained through a system relying on a combination of motor fuel and vehicle taxes, municipal bond issues, and, at the local level, general fund appropriations.

Today, that approach has reached the breaking point. America's surface transportation system is congested, travel times are uncertain, there is too little investment in transportation infrastructure, public spending has become politicized, and available infrastructure is old and deteriorating. In an age when electronic communications move at light speed, both passenger and freight movements are slowing, hindering the use of modern management techniques. As a result, motorists are frustrated and the economy is suffering. The traditional policy approach was appropriate for its time, but today it is failing the country.

The solution is not more of the same. Raising fuel taxes and funneling those revenues through the same political process will not revitalize America's transportation network. The solution instead lies in a better approach to U.S. transportation policy.

Fortunately, all the tools necessary for a change in course are currently available. The technology now exists to allow motorists to pay for road use with no traffic delays. Tolling technology is improving rapidly and its costs are declining to the point where it is almost free to the motorist. Its rate of adoption is accelerating, both in the United States and abroad. Moreover, acceptance of road pricing is rising, particularly when compared to attitudes toward higher fuel taxes. When motorists pay for the transportation services they receive, they will finally be treated like the customers they actually are, and providers will cater to their desires. Pricing allows a return to the user-pays principle on which fuel taxes were built.

Increased road pricing interacts with private participation in important ways. Although public-private partnerships can be and are used on unpriced facilities, the stream of payments generated by tolls can attract private investment to construct new facilities and renovate existing ones. A PPP ensures that toll revenue is used to maintain and operate the facility in question, but it also channels investment dollars toward those projects that are most valued by motorists rather than those that are most politically expedient. In short, private involvement will restore the link between the providers of a road, bridge, or tunnel and the motorists whom the facility is meant to serve.

PPPs encourage Americans to think of themselves as the owners of valuable transportation facilities, and to become active owners, like the shareholders of corporations, who insist that their appointed agents— whether they be governors, legislators, or transportation officials—operate, expand, and maintain their transportation facilities as efficiently as possible.

Public-sector partners must, however, consider a range of important issues prior to entering into a PPP, such as how monopoly power will be addressed, how concession length will be determined, and how the bidding process will be conducted. To be successful, the relationship must be carefully managed over the long term and adjusted as necessary to ensure that both partners benefit. Both the bidding process and ongoing contract management require expertise.

International experience with transportation PPPs is now vast. Private participation in transportation through public-private partnerships has been used in many countries for decades and in some, such as France, for centuries. PPPs have been successfully employed in Australia, Japan, Spain, Chile, Brazil, Portugal and many other countries for decades, and in U.S. transportation itself in the past. There is much experience from which to learn.

The climate for transportation PPPs in the United States is improving, with well over half the states adopting enabling legislation. Some states are already enjoying the benefits of PPPs, and other states should follow their lead. The high-powered incentives and fresh capital introduced by private participation represent a major step toward revitalizing

America's transportation system. If the benefits from that participation can be fully realized, then the U.S. transportation system will truly be on the road to renewal.

Notes

Preface

1. Network industries are usually defined as industries that have a fixed set of lines, pipes, or routes, with strong physical interconnections among component parts.

2. See NationalAtlas.gov, *Transportation of the United States*, http://www. national atlas.gov/transportation.html (accessed February 3, 2010).

3. See U.S. Department of Energy, "U.S. Transit Use Up, Driving Down in 2008," *EERE News*, March 11, 2009, http://apps1.eere.energy.gov/news/news_detail.cfm/news_id=12283 (accessed February 3, 2010).

Introduction

1. U.S. Department of Transportation, Office of Economic and Strategic Analysis, *Assessing the Full Costs of Congestion on Surface Transportation Systems and Reducing Them through Congestion Pricing*, February 2009, 47, http://ostpxweb.dot.gov/policy/reports/Costs%20of%20Surface%20Transportation%20Congestion.pdf (accessed February 4, 2010).

2. I use the terms "motorist" and "driver" throughout as shorthand for all transportation customers, including truckers, delivery companies, bus companies, and of course the drivers of passenger vehicles.

3. Texas Transportation Institute, "Economic Factors Tap the Brakes on Traffic Congestion," news release, July 8, 2009, http://mobility.tamu.edu/ums/media_ information/ press_release.stm (accessed February 4, 2010).

4. For example, Dr. Tim Sharp, clinical psychologist at the Happiness Institute in Sydney, Australia, states, "We...know that long commutes are very bad for happiness, so you could argue that things around roads, traffic and public transport could improve to minimize stress. People who have long commutes through peak hours tend to be less happy in their lives and work, but it's a complex area because people can't always find work close to home." Quoted in Peter Munro, "The Pursuit of Happiness," *Sunday Age*, August 2, 2009.

5. American Society of Civil Engineers, *2005 Infrastructure Report Card: Roads*, http://www.asce.org/reportcard/2005/page.cfm?id=30&printer=1 (accessed February 8, 2010).

6. American Association of State Highway and Transportation Officials/National Transportation Research Group, *Rough Roads Ahead: Fix Them Now or Pay for It Later*, 2009, http://roughroads.transportation.org/RoughRoads_FullReport.pdf (accessed August 13, 2009).

7. At the federal level, transportation earmarks are provisions in bills reauthorizing spending, whereby Congress directs funds to specific projects in specific locations, and often to the recipient of particular spending. The "bridge to nowhere" in Alaska was to be included in the 2006 National Appropriations Bill. It was projected to cost $398 million and would have connected the town of Ketchikan (population 8,900) to its airport on the Island of Gravina (population 50). The island was served by a ferry. See Ronald D. Utt, "The Bridge to Nowhere: A National Embarrassment," Heritage Foundation WebMemo no. 889, October 20, 2005, http://www.heritage.org/Research/Budget/wm889.cfm (accessed February 4, 2010). Although the amount of money allocated for use by Alaska was unchanged, the earmark was removed from the spending bill. See Carl Hulse, "Two 'Bridges to Nowhere' Tumble Down in Congress," *New York Times*, November 17, 2005. The many other examples of wasteful earmarks include the Bud Schuster Highway in Pennsylvania, which carries very little traffic and was enormously expensive to build. See Tad DeHaven, "The Timely Lesson of the 'Bud Schuster Highway,'" Cato@Liberty, January 7, 2009, http://www.cato-at-liberty.org/2009/01/07/the-timely-lesson-of-the-bud-shuster-highway (accessed April 6, 2010).

8. Samuel Staley and Adrian Moore, "Making Sure Infrastructure Stimulus Isn't Pork Parade," *Reason Foundation News Report*, January 7, 2009, http://reason.org/news/show/1003220.html (accessed February 4, 2010); and Source Watch, *Earmarks*, http://www.sourcewatch.org/index.php?title=Earmarks (accessed September 2, 2010).

9. U.S. Department of Transportation, *Review of Congressional Earmarks within Department of Transportation Programs*, report no. AV-2007-066, September 7, 2007, 4, http://www.oig.dot.gov/sites/dot/files/pdfdocs/Congressial_Earmarks-_AV-2007-66----508_Compliant.pdf (accessed September 1, 2009).

10. Matt Sundeen and James B. Reed, *Surface Transportation Funding Options for States* (Washington, DC: National Conference of State Legislatures, 2006), 25–26.

11. U.S. Department of Transportation, *Refocus. Reform. Renew.: A New Transportation Approach for America*, 2008, 9, http://www.atssa.com/galleries/default-file/RefocusReformRenew.pdf (accessed December 10, 2008).

Chapter 1: Three Critical Transportation Policy Reforms

1. National Surface Transportation Policy and Revenue Study Commission, *Transportation for Tomorrow: Report of the National Surface Transportation Policy and Revenue Study Commission*, December 2007, vol. 2, chap. 5, exhibit 5-2, http:// transportationfortomorrow.com./final_report/pdfvolume_2_chapter_5.pdf (accessed September 1, 2009); and U.S. Department of Transportation, *Refocus. Reform. Renew.: A New Transportation Approach for America*, 2008, 10, http://www. atssa.com/galleries/default-file/RefocusReformRenew.pdf (accessed December 10, 2008).

2. U.S. Department of Transportation, Federal Highway Administration, *Status of the Nation's Highways, Bridges, and Transit: 2006 Conditions and Performance*, 2006, chapter 6, http://www.fhwa.dot.gov/policy/2006cpr/es06h.htm (accessed September 1, 2009).

3. See, for example, Traffic World, "Questions and Answers with Transportation Secretary Mary E. Peters," July 7, 2008, 8, http://www.trafficworld-digital.com/ trafficworld/20080707/?pg=8 (accessed September 1, 2009); and Peter Samuel, "U.S. Sec. Peters to Governors: Toll Approach Will Unleash New Wave of Transport Investment," *TOLLROADSnews*, February 25, 2008. Also see Chairman of the Council of Economic Advisers, "The Nation's Infrastructure," in *Economic Report of the President* (Washington, DC: U.S. Government Printing Office, 2008), 151.

4. U.S. Department of Transportation, Federal Highway Administration, "Federal Tax Rates on Motor Fuels and Lubricating Oil," October 2002, http://www.fhwa.dot.gov/ohim/hs01/pdf/fe101a.pdf (accessed February 5, 2010).

5. MSNBC, "Obama Unveils MPG Rule, Gets Broad Support," May 19, 2009, http://www.msnbc.msn.com/id/30810514 (accessed February 5, 2010).

6. Robert Guy Matthews, "Fuel-Efficient Cars Dent States' Road Budgets," *Wall Street Journal*, April 25, 2007.

7. See U.S. Department of Energy, Energy Information Administration, *U.S. Retail Gasoline Prices*, http://www.eia.doe.gov/oil_gas/petroleum/data_publications/ wrgp/mogas_home_page.html (accessed August 20, 2009).

8. U.S. Department of Transportation, *Innovation Wave: An Update on the Burgeoning Private Sector Role in U.S. Highway and Transit Infrastructure*, 2008, 51, http://www.fhwa.dot.gov/reports/pppwave/ppp_innovation_wave.pdf (accessed September 1, 2009).

9. See David Stout, "Federal Highway Fund Running Out of Money," *New York Times*, September 6, 2008.

10. U.S. Department of Transportation, *Refocus. Reform. Renew.*, 11; U.S. Government Accountability Office, *Highway Public-Private Partnerships: More Rigorous Up-front Analysis Could Better Secure Potential Benefits and Protect the Public Interest*, GAO-08-44, 2008, 1, http://www.gao.gov/new.items/d0844.pdf

(accessed September 1, 2009); and Christopher Conkey, "U.S. Highway Fund Low on Cash Again," *Wall Street Journal*, June 3, 2009.

11. Robert T. Dunphy, "House Approve $7 Billion for Highway Trust Fund," Urban Land Institute, The Ground Floor blog, July 31, 2009, http://theground floor.typepad.com/the_ground_floor/2009/07/house-approve-7-billion-for-highway-trust-fund.html (accessed February 5, 2010).

12. Former secretary of transportation James H. Burnley stressed: "What worries me is that the whole concept of the trust fund is breaking down. You can't make the argument with a straight face that the trust fund should be spent just on transportation programs and that it should be walled off from the appropriations process while at the same time getting huge sums of money from general revenues. That is a corrosive process. By 2013, we could find the whole notion of the trust fund obsolete." Quoted in Mark B. Solomon, "A Lobbyist's-Eye View of the Washington Transport Scene," DCVelocity, April 19, 2010, http://www.dcvelocity.com/articles/20100419 lobbyists_eye_view_of_the_transport_scene (May 24, 2010).

13. One can think of permutations, such as state-owned enterprises or bureaucratic control, but both are variations on political control. There is evidence that the U.S. Postal Service, for instance, is operated in the interest of politically effective groups, such as labor unions and large mailers. See, for example, R. Richard Geddes, *Saving the Mail* (Washington, DC: AEI Press, 2003).

14. On the importance and effects of tax salience in transportation, see Amy Finkelstein, "EZ-Tax: Tax Salience and Tax Rates," *Quarterly Journal of Economics* 124, no. 3 (2009): 969–1010.

15. National Surface Transportation Infrastructure Financing Commission, *Paying Our Way: A New Framework for Transportation Finance*, February 2009, 108, http://financecommission.dot.gov/Documents/NSTIF_Commission_Final_Report_Mar09FNL.pdf (accessed February 5, 2010).

16. John L. Mica, "Transportation Report: Rebuilding of I-35W Bridge Shows How to Cut Red Tape on Projects Nationwide," *The Hill*, June 16, 2009.

17. Many analysts support this strategy. See, for example, National Surface Transportation Infrastructure Financing Commission, *Paying Our Way*, 184.

18. James M. Whitty, Oregon's Mileage Fee Concept and Road User Fee Pilot Program: Final Report (Salem, OR: Oregon Department of Transportation, 2007), 6, http://www.oregon.gov/ODOT/HWY/RUFPP/docs/RUFPP_finalreport.pdf (accessed September 1, 2009).

19. Ibid. A similar tax has been suggested in New Hampshire. See Terry Bellamy, "Transportation Group Adopts Report," *News and Observer*, December 10, 2008.

20. James M. Whitty, *Oregon's Mileage Fee Concept*, 8.

21. See Peter Samuel, "Existing Vehicle Data Bus, Cellphone SMS Proposed for Nearterm VMT Charge," *TOLLROADSnews*, July 10, 2009, http://www.toll roadsnews.com/node/4256 (accessed August 12, 2009).

22. See Peter Samuel, "Caltrans Report Says Skymeter 'Substantially Better' than Straight-GPS," *TOLLROADSnews*, September 1, 2009, http://www.toll roadsnews.com/node/4330 (accessed September 4, 2009).

23. Mary Peters, "Toward a New Surface Transportation Economic Model" (working paper, U.S. Department of Transportation, Washington, DC, n.d.), 3, http://financecommission.dot.gov/Documents/TransportationIssues(2).doc (accessed September 1, 2009).

24. See Center for Public Policy Priorities, "Who Pays Texas Taxes?" *Policy Page*, no. 115 (February 20, 2001), http://www.cppp.org/files/7/pp115.pdf (accessed September 1, 2009). The Texas study used the Suits Index, which is a mathematical comparison of the percentage of taxes paid to the percentage of total income received. See, for example, *Wikipedia*, s.v. "Suits Index," http://en.wikipedia.org/wiki/Suits_index (accessed April 23, 2010).

25. Tax Foundation, *What Does America Think about Taxes? The 2007 Annual Survey of U.S. Attitudes on Tax and Wealth*, Special Report No. 154, April 2007, 5, http://www.taxfoundation.org/files/sr154.pdf (accessed September 1, 2009).

26. Although conceptually different, a similar issue arises in a brownfield PPP, where citizens receive an upfront concession payment. As I discuss later in the book, a critical benefit of a greenfield PPP is that it provides a contractual guarantee that the tolls motorists pay will be used on that facility. The potential for diversion is greatly reduced.

27. There is now a vast academic literature on congestion pricing. William Vickrey, the 1996 Nobel laureate in economics, is considered the intellectual father of congestion pricing and has published widely on the topic. For a summary, see, for example, William Vickrey, quoted in "Principles of Efficient Congestion Pricing," Columbia University, June 1992, http://www.vtpi.org/vickrey.htm (accessed February 8, 2010). For a more recent contribution, see Anthony Downs, *Still Stuck in Traffic* (Washington, DC: Brookings Institution, 2004). I highlight only a few issues here to enhance the reader's appreciation of the interactions between congestion pricing and private investor participation.

28. U.S. Department of Transportation, Federal Highway Administration, *Congestion Pricing: A Primer*, publication no. FHWA-HOP-07-074, December 2006, 1, http://ops.fhwa.dot.gov/publications/congestionpricing/congestionpricing.pdf (accessed February 5, 2010).

29. Michael H. Schuitema, "Road Pricing as a Solution to the Harms of Traffic Congestion," *Transportation Law Journal* 34, no. 1 (2007): 103–104.

30. James M. Whitty, *Oregon's Mileage Fee Concept*, vi.

31. U.S. General Accounting Office, *Reducing Congestion: Congestion Pricing Has Promise for Improving Use of Transportation Infrastructure*, GAO-03-735T, 2003, 1, http://www.gao.gov/new.items/d03735t.pdf (accessed September 1, 2009).

32. See Michael H. Schuitema, "Road Pricing as Solution," 100.

33. Timothy D. Hau, "Congestion Pricing and Road Investment," in *Road Pricing, Traffic Congestion and the Environment: Issues of Efficiency and Social Feasibility,*

ed. Kenneth J. Button and Erik T. Verheof (Cheltenham, UK: Edward Elgar, 1998), 56.

34. See Robert Poole, "Bridges to Somewhere," *Surface Transportation Innovations*, no. 64 (February 11, 2009), http://reason.org/news/show/surface-transportation-innovat-63#feature1 (accessed September 1, 2009). Also, according to Timothy D. Hau, "The existence of economic profit serves as a surrogate market signal to expand capacity. …Similarly, if a road loses money, it suggests that planners may either have invested mistakenly or made overoptimistic forecasts of travel demand, for instance." See Hau, "Congestion Pricing and Road Investment," 56.

35. Douglas Holtz-Eakin (director, Congressional Budget Office), *Congestion Pricing for Highways*, statement before the U.S. Congress Joint Economic Committee, May 6, 2003, http://www.cbo.gov/doc.cfm?index=4197&type=0 (accessed September 1, 2009).

36. Chairman of the Council of Economic Advisers, *Economic Report of the President* (Washington, DC: U.S. Government Printing Office, 2007), 142.

37. Alan Day, "The Case for Road Pricing," *Economic Affairs* 18, no. 4 (December 1998): 5–8.

38. Milton Friedman and Daniel J. Boorstin, "How to Plan and Pay for the Safe and Adequate Highways We Need," in *Roads in a Market Economy*, ed. Gabriel Roth (Brookfield, VT: Aldershot, 1996), 223.

39. Sam Peltzman, "Pricing in Public and Private Enterprises: Electric Utilities in the United States," *Journal of Law and Economics* 14, no. 1 (1971): 109–47.

40. U.S. Government Accountability Office, *Highway Public-Private Partnerships*, 24–25.

Chapter 2: Basics of Public-Private Partnerships

1. Daniel B. Klein and John Majewski, "America's Toll Road Heritage: The Achievements of Private Initiative in the 19th Century," in *Street Smart: Competition, Entrepreneurship, and the Future of Roads*, ed. Gabriel Roth (New Brunswick, NJ: Transaction Publishers, 2006).

2. See Robert E. Wright and Brian P. Murphy, "The Private Provision of Transportation Infrastructure in Antebellum America: Lessons and Warnings," SSRN Working Paper, January 2009, table 1, "Number of Transportation Corporations by State and Decade," http://papers.ssrn.com/sol3/papers.cfm?abstract_id= 1335301 (accessed February 9, 2010).

3. National Surface Transportation Infrastructure Financing Commission, *Paying Our Way: A New Framework for Transportation Finance*, February 2009, 173, http://financecommission.dot.gov/Documents/NSTIF_Commission_Final_Report _Mar09FNL.pdf (accessed February 5, 2010).

4. U.S. Government Accountability Office, *Highway Public-Private Partnerships: More Rigorous Up-front Analysis Could Better Secure Potential Benefits and Protect the*

Public Interest, GAO-08-44, 2008, 5, http://www.gao.gov/new.items/ d0844.pdf (accessed September 1, 2009).

5. See U.S. Department of Transportation, Federal Highway Administration, "P3 Defined," http://www.fhwa.dot.gov/ipd/p3/defined/index.htm (accessed September 2, 2010).

6. The Ambassador Bridge linking the United States and Canada in Detroit, dating to the late 1920s, provides a historical example of a bridge privately owned from its beginnings. See "History: Ambassador Bridge," http://www. ambassadorbridge.com/history/index.html (accessed August 18, 2009). I was unable to find any historical examples in the United States of ownership changes from public to private. Actual private ownership does not appear to present problems in practice, however, as transport PPPs in Australia operate effectively under build-own-operate-transfer (BOOT) arrangements.

7. These categories are approximations. As the Federal Highway Administration puts it, "One man's BOOT (build-own-operate-transfer) is another's DBFO (design-build-finance-operate). The definitions, acronyms, and nomenclature used worldwide for PPPs are far from standard." U.S. Department of Transportation, Federal Highway Administration, *Public-Private Partnerships for Highway Infrastructure: Capitalizing on International Experience*, 2009, 3, http://international.fhwa.dot. gov/pubs/pl09010/pl09010.pdf (accessed September 1, 2009).

8. Congressional Budget Office, *Innovative Financing of Highways: An Analysis of Proposals*, 1998, 47, http://www.cbo.gov/ftpdocs/3xx/doc320/finhways.pdf (accessed September 1, 2009).

9. U.S. Department of Transportation, Federal Highway Administration, "Introduction," in *The Selective Use of Shadow Tolls in the United States*, http:// www.fhwa.dot.gov/innovativefinance/shadtoll.htm (accessed February 9, 2010).

10. Silviu Dochia and Michael Parker, *Introduction to Public-Private Partnerships with Availability Payments* (Philadelphia, PA: Jeffrey A. Parker and Associates Inc., 2009), http://www.transportationfinance.org/pdf/funding_financing/financing/jpa_ introduction_to_availability_payments_0709.pdf (accessed February 9, 2010).

11. U.S. Department of Transportation, Federal Highway Administration, Office of Innovative Program Delivery, "Case Studies: I-595 Corridor Roadway Improvements," http://www.fhwa.dot.gov/ipd/case_studies/fl_i595.htm (accessed September 2, 2010).

12. Ibid.

13. See Robert Poole, "The (Limited) Case for Shadow Tolling," Reason Foundation, March 1, 2007, http://reason.org/news/show/ 1002808.html (accessed July 27, 2009).

14. California Department of Transportation, "Toll Road Fact Sheet: State Route 91 (Orange County) 91 Express Lanes," 2009, http://www.dot.ca.gov/hq/ paffairs/about/toll/status.htm (accessed February 9, 2010).

15. See U.S. Department of Transportation, Federal Highway Administration, *Excellence in Highway Design: Category 8-Public/Private Participation*, 2003, http://wwwcf.fhwa.dot.gov/eihd/91exp.htm (accessed September 2, 2010).

16. See California State Senate, *Tolls, User Fees, and Public-Private Partnerships: The Future of Transportation Finance in California?* Hearing before the Transportation and Housing Committee, January 17, 2007, 7, http://republicans.transportation. house.gov/Media/File/Testimony/Highways/5-24-07-Lowenthal2.pdf (accessed February 9, 2010).

17. Nicholas Hann, *PPPs in North America—A Private Sector Partner's Perspective*, Maquarie North America Ltd., December 2006, http://csgb.ubc.ca/files/workshop 06/Region4-Hann.pdf (accessed February 10, 2010).

18. U.S. Department of Transportation, Federal Highway Administration, Office of Innovative Program Delivery, "Case Studies: Chicago Skyway," http://www.fhwa. dot.gov/ipd/case_studies/il_chicago_Skyway.htm (accessed February 10, 2010).

19. Peter Samuel, *Should States Sell Their Toll Roads?* Reason Foundation Policy Study 334, June 2, 2005, 11, http://reason.org/news/show/12767.htm (accessed September 1, 2009).

20. Ibid.

21. Leonard C. Gilroy, *Public-Private Partnerships in Transportation: Opportunities for Massachusetts*, testimony before the Massachusetts Joint Committee on Transportation, December 3, 2008, http://reason.org/news/show/public-private-partnerships-in-2 (accessed September 1, 2009).

22. Peter Samuel, *Should States Sell Their Toll Roads?*, 10.

23. Ibid.

24. The Indiana Toll Road brownfield concession discussed below did a better job on this score by precommitting to use the proceeds to fund the Major Moves transportation program, also discussed below.

25. NewEurope, "Portuguese, Brazilian Toll Operators Ink Road Lease," September 8, 2007, http://www.neurope.eu/articles/Portuguese-Brazilian-toll-operators-ink-road-lease/77383.php (accessed February 10, 2010).

26. See Dulles Greenway, "Facts and Myths," http://dullesgreenway.com/facts-myths.html (accessed September 5, 2009).

27. Ibid.

28. Ibid.

29. U.S. Department of Transportation, Federal Highway Administration, Office of Innovative Program Delivery, "PPP Case Studies: Dulles Greenway," http://www.fhwa.dot.gov/PPP/case_studies_dulles.htm (accessed September 5, 2009). The change in contract length suggests how this variable can be adjusted to account for differing financial conditions.

30. See Autostrade S.p.A., "Dulles Greenway Toll Road—Washington Area, Virginia," 2006, http://www.autostrade.it/en/gruppo/attinternaz_pres_dulles.html?init Pos=1 (accessed February 10, 2010).

31. U.S. Department of Transportation, Federal Highway Administration, Office of Innovative Program Delivery, "Case Studies: Indiana Toll Road," http:// www. fhwa.dot.gov/ipd/case_studies/in_indianatoll.htm (accessed February 10, 2010).

32. Leonard C. Gilroy, *Public-Private Partnerships in Transportation*.

33. Ibid.

34. Transurban, "The Capital Beltway Hot Lanes Project," http://www.transurban. com.au/transurban_online/tu_nav_black.nsf/v/73FE3C8EC263982CCA2572F30 0080DBD/$file/capital%20beltway%20final.pdf (accessed February 10, 2010).

35. U.S. Department of Transportation, Federal Highway Administration, Office of Innovative Program Delivery, "Case Studies: I-495 Capital Beltway HOT Lanes," http://www.fhwa.dot.gov/ipd/case_studies/va_capital_beltway.htm (accessed February 10, 2010).

36. Virginia Department of Transportation, "Hot Lanes Construction," http:// virginiahotlanes.com (accessed August 13, 2009).

37. Virginia Department of Transportation, Fluor Enterprises Inc., and Transurban (USA) Inc., "Comprehensive Agreement to Develop, Design, Finance, Construct, Maintain and Operate the Route 495 HOT Lanes in Virginia," April 28, 2005, 2, http://virginiahotlanes.com/documents/Comprehensive%20Agreement.pdf (accessed February 10, 2010).

38. U.S. Department of Transportation, Federal Highway Administration, "Capital Beltway HOT Lanes Project," September 2008, http://www.fhwa.dot.gov/ programadmin/contracts/sep14va2008.cfm (accessed September 6, 2010).

39. See Federal Highway Administration, Office of Innovative Program Delivery, "PPP Case Studies."

40. For example, according to Leonard C. Gilroy, director of government reform at the Reason Foundation, "In return for a 75-year concession, a private consortium is now adding the first new lanes to the I-495 Capital Beltway in Northern Virginia, which again is something government had been unable to implement through traditional funding approaches." See Pennsylvania House Republican Policy Committee, *Modernizing and Expanding Pennsylvania's Transportation Infrastructure through Public-Private Partnerships*, testimony of Leonard C. Gilroy, December 14, 2009, 7, http://reason.org/files/testimony_pennsylvania_transportation_public_ private_partnerships.pdf (accessed February 11, 2010). The PPP benefit of moving projects forward that would otherwise languish under traditional financing approaches is one of this book's recurring themes.

41. Wikipedia, s.v. "Texas State Highway 130," http://en.wikipedia.org/wiki/ Texas_State_Highway_130 (accessed August 12, 2009).

42. Round Rock, Texas, Chamber of Commerce, "Transportation," http://www. roundrockchamber.org/Transportation.67.0.html (accessed February 10, 2010).

43. Robert Poole, "A Tale of Two Texas Toll Roads: What's Really at Stake in the Battle Over SH-121," Reason Foundation, May 11, 2007, http://reason.org/news/ show/a-tale-of-two-texas-toll-roads (accessed August 12, 2009).

44. Pennsylvania House Republican Policy Committee, *Modernizing and Expanding Pennsylvania's Transportation Infrastructure through Public-Private Partnerships*, 6–7.

Chapter 3: Compared to What?
Why Private Investor Participation Is Needed

1. The World Bank defines SOEs as "government owned or government controlled economic entities that generate the bulk of their revenues from selling goods and services." World Bank, *Bureaucrats in Business: The Economics and Politics of Government Ownership* (Oxford: Oxford University Press, 1995), 26.

2. For excellent discussions of the principal-agent problem in various organizations, see Eugene F. Fama and Michael C. Jensen, "Separation of Ownership and Control," *Journal of Law and Economics* 26, no. 2 (1983): 301–25; and Eugene F. Fama and Michael C. Jensen, "Agency Problems and Residual Claims," *Journal of Law and Economics* 26, no. 2 (1983): 327–49.

3. See World Bank, *Bureaucrats in Business*, 3.

4. See Harold Demsetz and Kenneth Lehn, "The Structure of Corporate Ownership: Causes and Consequences," *Journal of Political Economy* 93, no. 6 (1985): 1155–77. Notably, other forms of private participation, such as through private equity, also typically result in highly concentrated, active ownership.

5. I use the term "captive equity holders" to capture this lack of tradability and pricing, as discussed below.

6. For a discussion of the difficulties involved in tying incentives for government firm managers to the effects of their decisions, see Andrei Shleifer, "State versus Private Ownership," *Journal of Economic Perspectives* 12, no. 4 (1998): 133–50.

7. For a comparison of governance mechanisms in postal service SOEs and private firms, see R. Richard Geddes, "Agency Costs and Governance in the U.S. Postal Service," in *Governing the Postal Service*, ed. J. Gregory Sidak (Washington DC: AEI Press), 1994.

8. In a publicly traded corporation, in contrast, shareholders can accumulate votes by accumulating shares, which gives them the incentive to overcome this "rational ignorance" problem of being uninformed in proxy vote matters. See, e.g., Frank H. Easterbrook and Daniel R. Fischel, "Voting," in *The Economic Structure of Corporate Law* (Cambridge: Harvard University Press, 1996).

9. This is in contrast to the "soft" incentives generated by firms that do not have a clearly defined group of owners, such as state-owned or nonprofit enterprises.

10. For an excellent discussion of the important role of owner homogeneity in the large corporation, see Henry Hansmann, *The Ownership of Enterprise* (Cambridge, MA: Harvard University Press, 1996).

11. This assumes that regulation is implemented properly in those cases where it is warranted to constrain monopoly power. I address those issues in chapter 8.

12. Chris Meads and Bryce Wilkinson, *Options for the Reform of Roading in New Zealand* (Wellington, New Zealand: CS First Boston, 1993).

13. The rapid adoption of electronic tolling technology by the private concessionaire on the Chicago Skyway is consistent with this assessment.

14. National Surface Transportation Infrastructure Financing Commission, *Paying Our Way: A New Framework for Transportation Finance,* February 2009, 177, http://financecommission.dot.gov/Documents/NSTIF_Commission_Final_Report _Mar09FNL.pdf (accessed February 5, 2010).

15. Peter Samuel, "Massachusetts Governor Will Argue Executive Power to Remove Turnpike's Amorello," *TOLLROADSnews*, March 17, 2005, http://www. tollroadsnews.com/node/1057 (accessed October 2, 2009).

16. See, for example, Section 141(k) of the *Delaware General Corporation Law.*

17. Peter Samuel, "Amorello Resigns—Gov Gives Him 6 Months Pay," *TOLLROADSnews*, March 17, 2005, http://www.tollroadsnews.com/node/1568 (accessed September 2, 2009).

18. See Peter Samuel, *Should States Sell Their Toll Roads?* Reason Foundation Policy Study 334, June 1, 2005, 2, http://reason.org/news/show/12767.htm (accessed September 1, 2009).

19. Commonwealth of Pennsylvania Department of Transportation, Pennsylvania Turnpike Commission, *Response to Request for Expression of Interest,* December 22, 2006, 6, quoting Op. Atty Gen. Pa. 16 at 6 (1990), http://www.paturnpike.com/ PPP/PPPINT/pdf/TurnpikeRFIResponse2.DOC (accessed October 29, 2009).

20. William Keisling, *Helping Hands: Illegal Political Corruption in Pennsylvania and at the Pennsylvania Turnpike* (Harrisburg, PA: Yardbird Books, 1995), 2.

21. William Keisling, *When the Levee Breaks: The Patronage Crisis at the Pennsylvania Turnpike, the General Assembly and the State Supreme Court* (Harrisburg, PA: Yardbird Books, 1993), 6.

22. Robert Caro, *The Power Broker: Robert Moses and the Fall of New York* (New York: Random House, 1974), 13.

23. Ibid., 15–16.

Chapter 4: Benefits of PPPs:
Competition, Management, and Project Delivery

1. I am grateful to the Edison Electric Institute for providing these data. Generation is based on owner's share of nameplate capacity, while transmission and distribution capacity are both based on circuit miles.

2. Charles Augustine, Bob Broxson, and Steven Peterson, *Understanding Natural Gas Markets*, Lexecon, 2006, http://www.api.org/aboutoilgas/upload/understanding_ natural_gas_markets.pdf (accessed November 19, 2008).

3. See, for example, James Gattuso and Norbert Michel, "Are U.S. Telecom Networks Public Property?" Backgrounder #1745 (Washington, DC: Heritage Foundation, 2004).

4. This ignores the possible creation of institutional arrangements in transportation that encourage competition among government entities. I am unaware of any such institutional arrangements.

5. For summaries of the social costs of monopoly, see Dennis W. Carlton and Jeffrey M. Perloff, *Modern Industrial Organization*, 2d ed. (New York: Harper Collins, 1994), 143–47, or W. Kip Viscusi, Joseph E. Harrington, and John M. Vernon, *Economics of Regulation and Antitrust*, 4th ed. (Cambridge: MIT Press, 2005), 88–92. For evidence on the social gains from introducing competition in network industries, especially transportation, see Clifford Winston, "U.S. Industry Adjustment to Economic Deregulation," *Journal of Economic Perspectives* 12, no. 3 (1998): 89–110; and Clifford Winston, "Economic Deregulation: Days of Reckoning for Microeconomists," *Journal of Economic Literature* 31 (1993): 1263–89. Moreover, there is evidence that state-owned enterprises will also exploit monopoly power. See, e.g., R. Richard Geddes, "Pricing by State-Owned Enterprises: The Case of Postal Services," *Managerial and Decision Economics* 29 (2008): 575–91.

6. See Edwin Chadwick, "Results of Different Principles of Legislation and Administration in Europe; of Competition for the Field, as Compared with Competition within the Field, for Service," *Journal of the Statistical Society of London* 22 (1859): 381–420.

7. Harold Demsetz, "Why Regulate Utilities?" *Journal of Law and Economics* 11 (1968): 55–65. For a discussion of the voluminous literature extending this concept and recent applications, see Viscusi et al., "Natural Monopoly Regulation and Electric Power," chap. 12, and "Franchise Bidding and Cable Television," chap. 13, in *Economics of Regulation*. The term "franchise bidding" may not be appropriate for contracts in which the private partner does not operate a facility for a meaningful period of time. Design-build contracts involve bidding by private partners but do not involve a term of franchise.

8. Here the per-unit cost is the cost to the bidder per vehicle using the facility. This statement is subject to several complications based on the number of bidders. See, for example, Viscusi et al., *Economics of Regulation*, 466. This is not to say that the price will be allocatively efficient, since price will not be set equal to marginal cost if the industry is characterized by increasing returns to scale. Rather, price will be set equal to average cost if there is a single product. See Lester G. Telser, "On the Regulation of Industry: A Note," *Journal of Political Economy* 77, no. 6 (1969): 937–52.

9. See, for example, Ronald M. Harstad and Michael A. Crew, "Franchise Bidding without Holdups: Utility Regulation with Efficient Pricing and Choice of Provider," *Journal of Regulatory Economics* 15 (1999): 141–63.

10. For a description of this approach, see Eduardo Engel, Ronald Fischer, and Alexander Galetovic, "Privatizing Roads: A New Method for Auctioning Highways," *Public Policy for the Private Sector*, note no. 112, World Bank Group, 1997, http://rru.worldbank.org/Documents/Toolkits/Highways/pdf/20a.pdf (accessed September 2, 2009).

11. See, for example, Darrin Grimsey and Mervyn K. Lewis, "Are Public Private Partnerships Value for Money? Evaluating Alternative Approaches and Comparing Academic and Practitioner Views," *Accounting Forum* 29, no. 4 (December 2005): 345–78.

12. The value of VfM tests driven by the PPP process was emphasized in a January 2010 study of Canadian PPPs, which tells us that "VfM tests are not undertaken as an afterthought: A first pass at the test is done before the start of the procurement process (i.e., before the request-for-proposal stage), and the test is finalized after the financial close. This report also suggests that there is value in updating the VfM studies ex post at key milestones, such as at completion of construction, and periodically thereafter. *In contrast, conventional infrastructure procurements are normally not subject to any VfM-type test to inform procurement strategy* (emphasis added)." See Conference Board of Canada, *Dispelling the Myths: A Pan-Canadian Assessment of Public-Private Partnerships for Infrastructure Investments*, January 2010, iv, http://www.conferenceboard.ca/documents.aspx?did=3431 (accessed April 2, 2010).

13. National Surface Transportation Policy and Revenue Study Commission, *Transportation for Tomorrow: Report of the National Surface Transportation Policy and Revenue Study Commission*, December 2007, vol. 1, 11, http://transportationfor tomorrow.org/final_report/pdfvolume_2_chapter_5.pdf (accessed September 1, 2009). Policymakers agree with this view. See, for example, John L. Mica, "Transportation Report: Rebuilding of I-35W Bridge Shows How to Cut Red Tape on Projects Nationwide," *The Hill*, June 16, 2009, http://thehill.com/special-reports/transportation-and-infrastructure-june-2009 (accessed February 5, 2010).

14. U.S. Department of Transportation, *Innovation Wave: An Update on the Burgeoning Private Sector Role in U.S. Highway and Transit Infrastructure*, 2008, 51, http://www.fhwa.dor.gov/reports/pppwave/ppp_innovation_wave.pdf (accessed September 1, 2009).

15. U.S. Department of Transportation, *Report to Congress on Public-Private Partnerships*, December 2004, 48, http://www.fhwa.dot.gov/reports/pppdec2004/ pppdec2004 (accessed August 5, 2009).

16. Quoted in John L. Mica, "Transportation Report."

17. National Surface Transportation Policy and Revenue Study Commission, *Transportation for Tomorrow*, 13. Commentators have also noted that faster project completion reduces exposure to construction-cost risk. See the final report of the National Surface Transportation Infrastructure Financing Commission, *Paying Our Way: A New Framework for Transportation Finance*, February 2009, 177, http:// financecommission.dot.gov/Documents/NSTIF_Commission_Final_Report_ Mar09FNL.pdf (accessed February 5, 2010).

18. This approach is used in Australia, for example. See David Czerwinski and R. Richard Geddes, "Policy Issues in U.S. Transportation Public-Private Partnerships: Lessons from Australia," Mineta Transportation Institute, *MTI Report* 09–15 (July 2010).

19. See Darrin Grimsey and Mervyn K. Lewis, "Evaluating the Risks of Public Private Partnerships for Infrastructure Projects," *International Journal of Project Management* 20, no. 2 (2002): 107–18.

20. Ronald J. Daniels and Michael J. Trebilcock, "Private Provision of Public Infrastructure: An Organizational Analysis of the Next Privatization Frontier," *University of Toronto Law Review* 46, no. 3 (1996): 400.

21. Experience in Australia suggests that care should be taken in paying concession fees on greenfield projects. The Cross City Tunnel is a 2.1-kilometer east-west tunnel running under Sydney's central business district that opened to traffic in 2005. The consortium that built the tunnel, the Cross City Motorway Pty Ltd, paid a $97 million concession fee to the government of New South Wales, which was criticized for not structuring the PPP to lower tolls as much as possible, among other issues. See David Czerwinski and R. Richard Geddes, "Policy Issues in U.S. Transportation," for more details.

22. U.S. Government Accountability Office, *Highway Public-Private Partnerships: More Rigorous Up-front Analysis Could Better Secure Potential Benefits and Protect the Public Interest*, GAO-08-44, 2008, 20, http://www.gao.gov/new.items/d0844.pdf (accessed September 1, 2009).

23. Jennifer Steinhauer, "In Budget Crises, States Reluctantly Halt Road Projects," *New York Times*, December 23, 2008; and Floyd Norris, "Municipal Bonds Are in Big Trouble; Auctions Yield Chaos for Bonds," *Market Place*, February 20, 2008, http://groups.google.com/group/alt.politics.economics/browse_thread/thread/7f42 95e39c8d9ce7 (accessed February 15, 2010).

24. Allen Consulting Group, *Performance of PPPs and Traditional Procurement in Australia, Final Report*, November 30, 2007, http://www.ippp.org/TheAllen Group.pdf (accessed November 25, 2008).

25. Ken Orski, "News from the Transportation Front No. 13," *Innovation Briefs*, April 16, 2007, http://www.innobriefs.com/abstracts/index.html (accessed November 24, 2008).

26. Robert Poole, "Risk Transfer in Toll Road Concessions," *Surface Transportation Innovations* #78, Reason Foundation, April 30, 2010, http://reason.org/news/show/surface-transportation-april-2010 (accessed September 6, 2010).

27. Ronald J. Daniels and Michael J. Trebilcock, "Private Provision of Public Infrastructure," 380.

28. National Surface Transportation Infrastructure Financing Commission, *Paying Our Way*, 174.

29. Private-sector experts who help to manage CityLink in Melbourne, Australia, stated in an interview with me that the firm focuses explicitly on maximizing throughput. This is reflected in accident response times. The contract requires a maximum response time of 10 minutes for an accident in a running lane, but the actual average time is 4 minutes. For an accident in a nonrunning lane, the contract mandates a maximum of 40 minutes, but the actual average time is 7.5

minutes. Fast response times are aided by a Central Control Computer System that includes a state-of-the-art incident-management system. It allows automatic incident detection by real-time digital-image processing and automated response plans.

30. André de Palma and Robin Lindsey report, "As is well known, holding output and the behavior of competitors fixed, a profit-maximizing firm will minimize total costs, *inclusive of the costs borne by its customers*.... In the case of private roads, drivers are the customers and their costs include time delays and other costs due to congestion. Thus, private operators have an incentive to adopt congestion pricing" (emphasis in original). André de Palma and Robin Lindsey, "Private Roads, Competition, and Incentives to Adopt Time-Based Congestion Tolling," *Journal of Urban Economics* 52 (2002): 218.

31. Ibid., 218–19.

32. Similarly, the Government Accountability Office states that "highway public-private partnerships may also yield other potential benefits, such as management of assets in ways that may yield efficiencies in operations and lifecycle management that may reduce total project costs over a project's lifetime. For example, in 2004, [the Federal Highway Administration] reported that, in contrast to traditional highway contracting methods that have sometimes focused on costs of individual project segments, highway public-private partnerships have more flexibility to maximize the use of innovative technologies.... Foreign officials with whom we spoke also identified lifecycle costing and management as a primary benefit of highway public-private partnerships." U.S. Government Accountability Office, *Highway Public-Private Partnerships: More Rigorous Up-front Analysis*, 23.

33. According to the British report, "Partnerships enable the public sector to benefit from commercial dynamism, innovation and efficiencies, harnessed through the introduction of private sector investors who contribute their own capital, skills and experience. In this way, they provide better value for money, which means that, within the resources available, we can deliver more essential services and to a higher standard than would otherwise have been the case. On average, privately financed projects are delivering savings of 17% compared to public sector alternatives—this represents savings of £2 billion on a £12 billion programme, equivalent to 25 new hospitals or 130 new schools." See *Public Private Partnerships: The Government's Approach*, Stationery Office, London, 2000, 5, http://www.hm-treasury.gov.uk/d/80.pdf (accessed August 5, 2009).

34. See U.S. Secretary of Transportation, "Teens Talk to Teens about Traffic Safety," Fastlane: The Official Blog of the U.S. Secretary of Transportation, December 9, 2008, http://fastlane.dot.gov/2008/12/teens-talk-to-t.html (accessed December 19, 2008).

35. See Viscusi, et al. *Economics of Regulation*, 694, table 19.2.

36. See Rajesh Subramanian, "Motor Vehicle Traffic Crashes as a Leading Cause of Death in the United States, 2006," *Traffic Safety Facts Research Note*, October

2009, table 1, "Top 10 Leading Causes of Death in the United States for 2006, by Age Group," NHTSA's National Center for Statistics and Analysis, http://www-nrd. nhtsa.dot.gov/Pubs/811226.PDF (accessed February 17, 2010).

37. Pew Center on the States, *Driven by Dollars: What States Should Know When Considering Public-Private Partnerships to Fund Transportation*, 2009, 13, http://www.pewtrusts.org/uploadedFiles/wwwpewtrustsorg/Reports/State_policy/PA_Turnpike_FINAL_WEB.pdf (accessed September 2, 2009).

38. U.S. Government Accountability Office, *Highway Public-Private Partnerships*, 24.

39. See Pew Center on the States, *Grading the States: Pennsylvania*, 2008, http://www.pewcenteronthestates.org/uploadedFiles/Pennsylvania%20%20Governing%20article%202008.pdf (accessed February 17, 2010). See also Peter Samuel, *The Role of Tolls in Financing 21st Century Highways*, Reason Foundation Policy Study 359, May 1, 2007, 32, on the tendency of public authorities to defer maintenance when under fiscal pressure.

40. Bob Carr, "Good Roads Sooner: Public-Private Partnerships in New South Wales," in *Innovators in Action 2009*, Reason Foundation, http://reason.org/news/show/good-roads-sooner-public-priva (accessed February 24, 2010). Carr, a former Labor Party premier of the New South Wales government, also notes that, of the AUD$5.4 billion capital value of the six motorway projects opened around Sydney since 1996, AUD$4.6 billion was provided by the private sector, implying a capital cost to the government of only AUD$800 million (about $727 million in 2010).

41. Current state fiscal conditions have resulted in underpolicing in some states. In January 2010, only seven state troopers covered the entire state of Iowa overnight. Governor Mitchell E. Daniels Jr., "2010 State of the State Address," January 19, 2010, http://www.in.gov/gov/10stateofstate.htm (accessed February 18, 2010).

42. Sovereign immunity has been extended to states and their agencies, but often not to counties and municipalities. See, for example, *Lake Country Estates v. Tahoe Planning Agcy.*, 440 U.S. 391 (1979), 401. While the concession agreement may stipulate that legal liability continues to lie with the state, private operators cannot be protected by sovereign immunity.

43. See, for example, Richard A. Posner, *Economic Analysis of Law*, 4th ed. (Boston: Little, Brown, 1992), 163–75.

44. See, for example, Peter Appel, "New ITS Strategic Plan Envisions Unprecedented Mobility and Safety," Fast Lane: Official Blog of the U.S. Transportation Secretary, March 8, 2010, http://fastlane.dot.gov/2010/03/guest-blogger-dot-research-and-innovative-technology-administrator-peter-appel-new-its-strategic-pla.html (accessed March 10, 2010).

45. See Advanced Design Consulting USA Inc., "MEMS Concrete Monitoring System," http://www.adc9001.com/documents/ADC_2007_tech_brochure.pdf (accessed October 18, 2008).

46. See Linda Rodriguez McRobbie, "An EKG for Cracking Bridges," CNN Money, May 10, 2010, http://money.cnn.com/2010/05/10/smallbusiness/matech_bridges/ (accessed May 12, 2010).

47. Andrei Shleifer, "State versus Private Ownership," *Journal of Economic Perspectives* 12, no. 4 (1998): 138.

48. Ibid., 137.

49. Government Accountability Office, *Highway Public-Private Partnerships*, 24.

50. The International Roughness Index (IRI) was developed by the World Bank in the 1980s. It is a measure of surface roughness given by the number of inches per mile that a van-mounted laser jumps as it is driven over the road. The IRI rises with road roughness. See Pennsylvania Department of Transportation, "International Roughness Index," http://www.penndot8.com/iri.htm (accessed February 18, 2010).

51. Regarding KPIs, the Federal Highway Administration states, "Unquestionably, performance measures or key performance indicators (KPIs) are central to the most recent PPP projects observed in the nations the scan team visited.... For instance, Spain has used KPIs to manage safety, heavy vehicles, congestion, winter weather conditions, and toll collection times, as well as other elements." Referring to the EastLink project in Melbourne, the FHWA reports, "In Victoria, the KPIs associated with the EastLink project focus on customer service, road maintenance, landscape and environment, and tolling accuracy. Failure to comply with KPIs can result in up to $17 million annually in deductions for the PPP contracts. Any deductions collected from the concessionaire will be distributed to EastLink's users rather than retained by the government, since the users are the ones not receiving the paid for service." U.S. Department of Transportation, Federal Highway Administration, *Public-Private Partnerships for Highway Infrastructure: Capitalizing on International Experience,* 2009, 4, http://international.fhwa.dot.gov/pubs/pl09010/pl09010.pdf (accessed September 1, 2009).

52. For an example of how this is recognized by other researchers, see Ronald J. Daniels and Michael J. Trebilcock, "Private Provision of Public Infrastructure," 391–93.

53. Allen Consulting Group, *Performance of PPPs*, 1.

54. See Daniels and Trebilcock, "Private Provision," 388–89.

55. Government Accountability Office, *Highway Public-Private Partnerships*, 42.

56. Ibid.

57. See Leonard C. Gilroy, "Turnpike Lease a Better Deal for Taxpayers, Drivers," Reason Foundation, 2008, http://www.reason.org/commentaries/gilroy_200805 20.shtml (accessed October 29, 2008).

Chapter 5: Benefits of PPPs: Investment, Risk Transfer, and the Rationalization of Investment

1. See D. J. Gribbon, "Concession Agreements: The Key to Unlocking Capital," in *Horizon: The Future of Transportation* (Austin: Texas Department of Transportation, 2006), 16–22.

2. Peter Samuel, *The Role of Tolls in Financing 21st Century Highways*, Reason Foundation Policy Study 359, 2007, 29.

3. Equity allows leverage to be used. A typical mixture of equity and debt investment in a PPP is 40 percent equity and 60 percent debt, but the mixture varies across time and projects. See Government Accountability Office, *Highway Public-Private Partnerships: More Rigorous Up-front Analysis Could Better Secure Potential Benefits and Protect the Public Interest*, GAO-08-44, 2008, 28n22, http://www.gao.gov/new.items/d0844.pdf (accessed September 1, 2009). Also, according to D. J. Gribbon, "The traditional bond financing approach has layers of conservatism built into valuing the asset, and that conservatism tends to undervalue the asset." See D. J. Gribbon, "Understanding Contemporary Public-Private Highway Transactions: The Future of Infrastructure Finance," testimony before the U.S. House Transportation and Infrastructure Committee, Subcommittee on Highways, Transit, and Pipelines, May 24, 2006, 3.

4. National Surface Transportation Infrastructure Financing Commission, *Paying Our Way: A New Framework for Transportation Finance*, March 2009, 165, http://financecommission.dot.gov/Documents/NSTIF_Commission_Final_Report_Mar09FNL.pdf (accessed February 5, 2010).

5. Long-term contracting with the government is problematic even in such developed countries as Canada, however. See Ronald J. Daniels and Michael J. Trebilcock, "Private Provision of Public Infrastructure: An Organizational Analysis of the Next Privatization Frontier," *University of Toronto Law Review* 46, no. 3 (1996): 412.

6. See Rafael LaPorta, Florencio López-de-Silanes, and Andrei Shleifer, "The Economic Consequences of Legal Origins," *Journal of Economic Literature* 46, no. 2 (2008): 285–332 and the references cited there.

7. Private infrastructure investment may also attract a new type of bond investor because it offers primarily taxable bonds (private activity bonds, discussed below, being an exception). Investors who already enjoy favorable tax treatment may not find municipal bonds appealing but may be attracted to taxable infrastructure bonds.

8. An operator (either public or private) can, of course, take actions that reduce facility value, such as deferring maintenance. That is why enforceable, transparent contractual standards are so critical.

9. Pew Center on the States, *Driven by Dollars: What States Should Know When Considering Public-Private Partnerships to Fund Transportation*, 2009, 13,

http://www.pewtrusts.org/uploadedFiles/wwwpewtrustsorg/Reports/State_policy/PA_Turnpike_FINAL_WEB.pdf (accessed September 2, 2009).

10. See Robert Poole, "Pension Funds and Infrastructure Investment," Reason Foundation, May 1, 2008, http://reason.org/news/show/ 1003278.htm (accessed August 6, 2009).

11. See National Surface Transportation Infrastructure Financing Commission, *Paying Our Way*, 179: "Potential national security issues should be fully addressed by existing federal laws governing foreign investment in critical infrastructure."

12. Leonard C. Gilroy and Adam Summers, "Detailing Foreign Management of US Infrastructure," Reason Foundation, March 1, 2006, http://reason.org/news/show/detailing-foreign-management-o (accessed August 6, 2009).

13. The chapter entitled "Surface Transportation" in the Reason Foundation's 2009 annual privatization report cites a 2008 ranking of global PPP transportation infrastructure companies. Of the top ten, eight are European, one is Australian, and one is Chinese. U.S. companies appear only in the twenty-second, twenty-fourth, and twenty-seventh positions. Leonard C. Gilroy, ed., *Annual Privatization Report 2009*, Reason Foundation, http://reason.org/files/annual_privatization_report_2009.pdf (accessed April 20, 2010).

14. This highlights the confusion of those officials and analysts who, on the one hand, implore pension funds to invest more in U.S. infrastructure while, on the other, diminish the opportunity to do so by discouraging PPPs.

15. That is, earnings before interest, taxes, depreciation, and amortization, considered to be a measure of cash earnings.

16. See "A Problem of Access," *InfrastructureInvestor*, January 28, 2010, http://www.infrastructureinvestor.com/Article.aspx?article=50188 (accessed February 24, 2010).

17. As Georg Inderst writes, "The idea of investing in infrastructure seems to strike a chord with many pension plan directors and members. Infrastructure feels more 'tangible' and 'real' than a lot of other complex products and derivative strategies presented to pension funds these days, where they find it difficult to detect the underlying value. In addition, infrastructure is made for the long term, and there seems to be a natural fit with the long-term liabilities of many pension plans. For some people there is also a connotation to sustainable or socially responsible investing, which is an increasingly popular route chosen in particular by public and industry-wide pension plans." See Georg Inderst, "Pension Fund Investment in Infrastructure" (OECD Working Papers on Insurance and Private Pensions, no. 32, Organisation for Economic Co-operation and Development, 2009), 4, http://www.oecd.org/dataoecd/41/9/42052208.pdf (accessed March 1, 2010). Moreover, the Public-Private Infrastructure Advisory Facility, which was established by a joint effort of the governments of Japan and the United Kingdom in 1999, states that its mission is "to help eliminate poverty and achieve sustainable development through public-private partnerships in infrastructure." See Public-Private

Infrastructure Advisory Facility, "PPIAF's Mission," http://www.ppiaf.org/content/view/37/67 (accessed April 6, 2010).

18. This assumes that toll road operators choose to increase tolls at the rate of the cap. They may choose not to do so if traffic volumes fall substantially as tolls are increased, i.e., where the elasticity of demand is high due to many alternatives. I discuss this issue in more detail in chapter 8.

19. See, for example, Christina Currier, *Transportation Infrastructure Investment Opportunities for State Government Pension Plans* (Austin, TX: Texas Department of Transportation, Government and Business Enterprises Division, March 2007), 4–5, ftp://ftp.dot.state.tx.us/pub/txdot-info/gbe/pension_plan_wquote_032707.pdf (accessed October 15, 2009).

20. Pennsylvania Governor Rendell argued that the Office of Public Benefit "will have a chilling effect on private investment in infrastructure" at a time when such investment is needed most. See Cezary Podkul, "Penn Governor: Help Me Kill Office of Public Benefit," *InfrastructureInvestor*, September 30, 2009, http://www.infrastructureinvestor.com/Article.aspx?article=46197 (accessed November 1, 2010).

21. See, for example, U.S. Department of Transportation, Federal Highway Administration, Office of Innovative Program Delivery, "State P3 Legislation," http://www.fhwa.dot.gov/ipd/p3/state_legislation/index.htm (accessed February 24, 2010).

22. According to Mark Florian and colleagues, "For years, pension funds from Canada, Europe, and Australia have been investing in public infrastructure for both a steady return and for the long-lived nature of these assets." Mark Florian, Jeff Holt, and Jenn Frates, "Public-Private Partnerships: Examining the Key Drivers of Value," *Horizon: The Future of Transportation* (Austin, TX: Texas Department of Transportation, 2007), 5–6.

23. Leonard C. Gilroy, *Annual Privatization Report*, 55.

24. Ibid.

25. Kearsarge Global Advisors, *Benefits of Private Investment in Infrastructure*, PowerPoint presentation, March 2010, 5, http://www.slideshare.net/anxora/lobbyist-presentation-presentation (accessed April 27, 2010).

26. Leonard C. Gilroy, *Annual Privatization Report*, 55.

27. Georg Inderst, "Pension Fund Investment in Infrastructure," 13.

28. Kristen Paech, "Unlisted Infrastructure on Pension Fund Radar," Top1000funds.com, March 31, 2009, available at http://www.top1000funds.com/market-analysis/2009/03/31/unlisted-infrastructure-on-pension-fund-radar (accessed November 1, 2010).

29. Ibid.

30. Leonard C. Gilroy, *Annual Privatization Report*, 55.

31. Ibid.

32. See Andrew Sheen, "A Solid Route to Diversification," *Global Pensions*, March 4, 2008, http://globalpensions.com/showPage.html?page=gp_display_feature&temp PageId=725066 (accessed October 23, 2008).

33. Researchers have noted the risk-spreading benefits of listed infrastructure funds. According to Kevin Davis, for example, "Uncertainty about future revenues (around a given expected value) imposes risks on the owners of infrastructure assets. However, if those risks are spread over a sufficiently large group of investors, they may become insignificantly small in the context of the overall portfolio position of each investor. Thus, for example, creation of listed infrastructure 'trusts' enables both exit and recovery of capital (and realization of excess project returns) by original financiers of such assets, and spreading of risk over a wide range of investors." See Kevin Davis, "PPPs and Infrastructure Investment," *Australian Economic Review* 38, no. 4 (2005): 442.

34. See Georg Inderst, "Pension Fund Investment in Infrastructure," 8.

35. Vivian Marino, "Turning Infrastructure into Profits," *New York Times*, May 24, 2009.

36. For a detailed discussion of various risks associated with transport PPPs, see David Czerwinski and R. Richard Geddes, "Policy Issues."

37. U.S. Government Accountability Office, *Highway Public-Private Partnerships: More Rigorous Up-front Analysis*, 22.

38. Of course, future traffic flows must be estimated even for a brownfield PPP, so the risk-transfer benefits of a PPP associated with traffic flows obtain in the long run for brownfields, as well.

39. See Legislative Study Committee on Private Participation in Toll Roads, *Report of the Legislative Study Committee on Private Participation in Toll Projects*, 2008, 46, ftp://ftp.dot.state.tx.us/pub/txdot-info/library/pubs/bus/tta/sb_792_report.pdf (accessed September 2, 2009).

40. See ibid., 42–45, for a discussion of other overly optimistic traffic and revenue forecasts.

41. Darrin Grimsey and Mervyn K. Lewis, "Evaluating the Risks." Private investors are also able to protect themselves from many PPP risks by purchasing insurance through private companies.

42. Ibid.

43. See also U.S. Department of Transportation, Federal Highway Administration, *Public-Private Partnerships for Highway Infrastructure: Capitalizing on International Experience*, 2009, 21, http://international.fhwa.dot.gov/pubs/pl09010/pl09010.pdf (accessed September 1, 2009).

44. Darrin Grimsey and Mervyn K.Lewis, "Evaluating the Risks," 109.

45. In an April 2002 speech in Sydney, Australia, for example, John Pierce, the secretary of the New South Wales Treasury, emphasized optimal risk transfer: "Transferring risks to the private sector, where it is better placed than government to manage those risks, can further improve the cost and quality of infrastructure. Strong incentives for performance can be imposed by a performance-based

payment regime, such that the private sector's investment in a project is always at risk. The phrase 'where the private sector is better placed to manage risk' should be emphasized." New South Wales Treasury, Office of Financial Management, *Private Provision of Public Infrastructure and Services*, research and information paper, April 2002, 3, http://www.treasury.nsw.gov.au/__data/assets/pdf_file/0017/5390/trp02-3.pdf (accessed February 22, 2010).

46. Darrin Grimsey and Mervyn K.Lewis, "Evaluating the Risks," 111. Other divisions of risks are possible, such as operating risks versus financial risks.

47. However, my discussions with PPP experts in Australia indicate that the kinds of risks that the public sector will assume for a particular type of infrastructure are becoming more clearly defined over time. Private sector partners thus have a clearer idea of the risks they will be assuming and can price their bids appropriately.

48. Ronald J. Daniels and Michael J. Trebilcock, "Private Provision," 382n20.

49. New South Wales Treasury, Office of Financial Management, *Private Provision of Public Infrastructure and Services*, 3.

50. Scholars have recognized captive equity since at least the 1960s. See, for example, Armen Alchian, "Some Economics of Property Rights," *Il Politico* 30, no. 4 (1965): 816–29.

51. Others have recognized that placing risk on taxpayers hides the true cost of risk assumption. Kenneth Small, for example, states that "unlike a private risk premium, this social cost is not reflected in the observed market interest rates, because it is borne by taxpayers rather than investors. It implies that citizens are not willing to fund every public project that would appear to be warranted using market rates on government debt." Kenneth A. Small, "Private Provision of Highways: Economic Issues," *Transport Reviews* 30, no. 1 (January 2010): 14–15. A line of research argues that the social cost of risk bearing can be reduced by government financing. See, for example, L. P. Foldes and R. Rees, "A Note on the Arrow-Lind Theorem," *American Economic Review* 67, no. 2 (March 1977): 188–93. Both Michael Klein and Timothy Irwin show, however, that the true cost of capital is the risk-free interest rate plus a risk premium, where the risk premium depends only on project-specific risk rather than on who bears it. See Michael Klein, "The Risk Premium for Evaluating Public Projects," *Oxford Review of Economic Policy* 13, no. 4 (1997): 29–42; and Timothy C. Irwin, *Government Guarantees: Allocating and Valuing Risk in Privately Financed Infrastructure Projects* (Washington, DC: World Bank, 2007).

52. See, for example, Dennis J. Enright, "The Public versus Private Toll Road Choice," *Horizon: The Future of Transportation* (Austin, TX: Texas Department of Transportation, 2007), 14–22; and Commonwealth of Pennsylvania Department of Transportation, Pennsylvania Turnpike Commission, *Response to Request for Expression of Interest*, December 22, 2006, http://www.paturnpike.com/PPP/PPPINT/pdf/TurnpikeRFIResponse2.DOC (accessed October 29, 2009).

53. See Daniel B. Klein and John Majewski, "America's Toll Road Heritage: The Achievements of Private Initiative in the 19th Century," in *Street Smart: Competition,*

Entrepreneurship, and the Future of Roads, ed. Gabriel Roth (New Brunswick, NJ: Transaction Publishers, 2006), 278; and Daniel B. Klein and John Majewski, "Economy, Community, and Law: The Turnpike Movement in New York, 1797–1845," *Law and Society Review* 26, no. 3 (1993): 469–512.

54. Eduardo Engel, Ronald Fischer, and Alexander Galetovic, "Privatizing Highways in the United States," *Review of Industrial Organization* 29 (2006): 33.

55. Efriam Sadka, "Public-Private Partnerships—A Public Economics Perspective," *IMF Working Paper WP/06/77* (Washington, DC: The International Monetary Fund), 2006, 8.

56. See, for example, Philip A. Viton, "Private Roads," *Journal of Urban Economics* 37 (May 1995): 260–89.

57. It is, of course, critical that all such subsidies be completely transparent and justified on firm public policy grounds.

58. See the description of the selection of Stephenson Construction International (SCI) on the basis of the lowest required subsidy to construct the Prince Edward Island Fixed Link in U.S. Government Accountability Office, *Highway Public-Private Partnerships: More Rigorous Up-front Analysis*, 45. On the Canadian experience, see Daniels and Trebilcock, "Private Provision," 382.

59. U.S. Department of Transportation, Federal Highway Administration, *Public-Private Partnerships for Highway Infrastructure*, 19.

60. See Ronald J. Daniels and Michael J. Trebilcock, "Private Provision," 393. Notably, the incentives of the private provider to proceed with projects that have a positive net present value may be distorted by price regulation. See ibid.

61. In an example of time-inconsistent behavior, the government of New South Wales in Australia canceled a PPP metro project in Sydney's central business district even though the project was already under way. The government promised to reimburse bidders for "all reasonable costs incurred" in their bids, up to $100 million. See Andrew West, "All Roads Lead to the City," *Sydney Morning Herald* (Australia), February 22, 2010. Several commentators I interviewed stressed that this decision would stymie future private infrastructure investment in New South Wales since investors could no longer be sure that the government would follow through with proposed projects.

62. An approach that excludes private participation does not incur transaction costs since there is no contract. However, there will nevertheless be agency costs associated with monitoring and incentivizing managerial performance. Those costs are more difficult to observe and measure when they are internal to government.

63. Peter Kenter, "Infrastructure: The Debate over PPP Honoraria," *Journal of Commerce: Western Canada's Construction Newspaper,* December 6, 2006, http://www.joconl.com/article/id21895?search_term=honorarium (accessed March 31, 2010). This approach may not reduce the overall social costs of contracting, but it will make the process more competitive by increasing the number of bidders.

64. Ken Orski, "The Promise and Risks of Public-Private Partnerships," *Innovation Briefs* 21, no. 6 (April 5, 2010): 1.

65. See K & L Gates LLP, *Financing Business Expansion through Tax-Exempt Private Activity Bonds*, http://www.portofmoseslake.com/PDF%20Files/Financing %20Business%20Expansion%20by%20IDBs%20-Preston,%20Gates%20 &%20Ellis%20-2007.pdf (accessed February 19, 2010), from which this discussion borrows.

66. Michael Saunders, "The Role of PPPs in Addressing Congestion," *Public Roads* 71, no. 1 (July/August 2007), http://www.tfhrc.gov/pubrds/07july/04.htm (accessed March 1, 2010).

67. Robert Poole, "Some Good News for PPPs in Stimulus Bill," *Surface Transportation Innovations* 65, Reason Foundation, March 6, 2009, http://reason.org/newsletters/stinnovations/2009.html (accessed August 6, 2009).

68. Michael Saunders, "The Role of PPPs in Addressing Congestion."

69. As the Federal Highway Administration states, "Passage of the private activity bond legislation reflects the Federal Government's desire to increase private sector investment in U.S. transportation infrastructure. Providing private developers and operators with access to tax-exempt interest rates lowers the cost of capital significantly, enhancing investment prospects. Increasing the involvement of private investors in highway and freight projects generates new sources of money, ideas, and efficiency." See U.S. Department of Transportation, Federal Highway Administration, Office of Innovative Program Delivery, "Tools and Programs: Private Activity Bonds (PABs)," http://www.fhwa.dot.gov/ipd/p3/tools_programs/pabs.htm#current (accessed February 19, 2010).

70. Ibid.

71. U.S. Department of Transportation, Federal Highway Administration, Office of Innovative Program Delivery, "TIFIA Defined," http://www.fhwa.dot.gov/ipd/tifia/defined/index.htm (accessed May 26, 2010).

72. Michael Saunders, "The Role of PPPs in Addressing Congestion."

73. National Surface Transportation Infrastructure Financing Commission, *Paying Our Way*, 168. The report states that "TIFIA has proved to be a successful niche program to facilitate the financing of major projects with dedicated revenues, especially user-backed projects, by providing important credit enhancement." Ibid., 209.

74. The consequence of using the tax-exempt market is that revenue into the fund is used to pay off this debt, effectively converting an SIB into a state-financing conduit. National Surface Transportation Infrastructure Financing Commission, *Paying Our Way*, 169.

75. See Kenneth A. Small, "Private Provision of Highways," 13.

76. Evidence shows that PPPs also improve substantially the transparency of the procurement process over that of traditional approaches. The Conference Board of Canada states that "the procurement process for the second wave of [PPPs] is considerably more transparent than that for conventional infrastructure projects of equivalent scale. This is because the key procurement documentation, including a redacted form of the partnership contract, is publicly available and a fairness

commissioner assesses the fairness and transparency of the process for all bidders. Neither of these features is typical of conventional public infrastructure procurement." Conference Board of Canada, *Dispelling the Myths: A Pan-Canadian Assessment of Public-Private Partnerships for Infrastructure Investments*, January 2010, iv, http://www.conferenceboard.ca/documents.aspx?did=3431 (accessed April 2, 2010).

Chapter 6: The Benefits of Brownfield Public-Private Partnerships

1. Jeffrey N. Buxbaum and Iris N. Ortiz, *Public Sector Decision Making for Public-Private Partnerships: A Synthesis of Highway Practice*, Transportation Research Board, National Cooperative Highway Research Program, NCHRP Synthesis 391, 2009, nttp://onlinepubs.trb.org/onlinepubs/nchrp/nchrp_syn_391.pdf (accessed September 3, 2009).

2. This would have been the arrangement under the terms of the proposed Pennsylvania Turnpike lease. See, for example, Leonard C. Gilroy, "Turnpike Lease a Better Deal for Taxpayers, Drivers," Reason Foundation, May 20, 2008, http://www.reason.org/commentaries/gilroy_20080520.shtml (accessed October 29, 2008).

3. The Australian government's Productivity Commission states that "PPP use in Australia has…fostered the development of a large domestic infrastructure investment, construction, and facility operating industry." Australian Productivity Commission, "Public Infrastructure Financing: An International Perspective," Productivity Commission staff working paper by Chris Chan, Danny Forwood, Heather Roper, and Chris Sayers, March 2009, xxvii. Also see U.S. Department of Transportation, Federal Highway Administration, *Public-Private Partnerships for Highway Infrastructure: Capitalizing on International Experience*, 2009, 49, http://international.fhwa.dot.gov/pubs/pl09010/pl09010.pdf (accessed September 1, 2009).

4. Analysts have recognized this benefit. Deloitte Consulting, for example, states that "in addition to providing higher-quality infrastructure at lower cost, governments can use PPP transactions to unlock the value from undervalued and underutilized assets, such as land and buildings, and use those funds to help pay for new infrastructure." Deloitte Consulting, *Closing the Infrastructure Gap: The Role of Public-Private Partnerships*, 2006, 2, http://www.deloitte.com/dtt/cda/doc/content/us_ps_ClosingInfrastructureGap2006(1).pdf (accessed September 6, 2010).

5. For a discussion of the value of Postal Service assets, see Douglas K. Adie, "Organizational Choices," in *Monopoly Mail: Privatizing the U.S. Postal Service* (New Brunswick, NJ: Transaction Publishers, 1989).

6. See, for example, Bruce Gottlieb, "Why Do Investment Banks Go Public?" *Slate*, June 19, 1998, http://www.slate.com/id/1001946 (accessed December 23, 2008).

7. Peter Samuel, *The Role of Tolls in Financing 21st Century Highways*, Reason Foundation Policy Study 359, May 1, 2007, 29, http://reason.org/news/show/the-role-of-tolls-in-financing (accessed April 23, 2010).

8. Germá Bel and John Foote, "Tolls, Terms, and Public Interest in Road Concessions Privatization: A Comparative Analysis of Recent Transactions in the USA and France," *Transport Reviews* 29, no. 3 (2009): 397–413.

9. See Mary E. Peters, "Taking the Transportation Revolution to the States," Welcome to the Fast Lane: The Official Blog of the U.S. Secretary of Transportation, June 24, 2008, http://fastlane.dot.gov/secretarysblog/2008/06/taking-the-tran.html (accessed June 25, 2008).

10. See Peter Samuel, "Abertis/Citi Selected in $12.8 Billion Bid for Pennsylvania Turnpike Lease," *TOLLROADSnews*, May 19, 2008, http://www.tollroadsnews.com/node/3547 (accessed September 3, 2009). Unfortunately, Abertis allowed its bid to expire before the state legislature took action.

11. Many PPP projects are completed under a project-financing approach. Project financing is defined as "the creation of a legally independent project company financed with equity from one or more sponsoring firms and non-recourse debt for the purpose of investing in a capital asset." See Benjamin Esty, *An Overview of Project Finance and Infrastructure Finance–2006 Update* (Boston: Harvard Business School Publishing, 2007), 213. Australian PPP experts I interviewed stressed that the project financing approach leads investors to undertake careful due diligence prior to investing in a particular project.

Chapter 7: The Benefits of Private Investor Participation Demonstrated

1. William L. Megginson and Jeffry M. Netter, "From State to Market: A Survey of Empirical Studies on Privatization," *Journal of Economic Literature* 39 (2001): 380. The authors report that the state-owned enterprise share of global gross domestic product declined by almost half, from 10 percent in 1979 to less than 6 percent in 2001. It has surely declined further since then.

2. Ibid.

3. Conference Board of Canada, *Dispelling the Myths: A Pan-Canadian Assessment of Public-Private Partnerships for Infrastructure Investments*, January 2010, iii, http://www.conferenceboard.ca/documents.aspx?did=3431 (accessed April 2, 2010). The second wave of Canadian PPP projects refers to those that occurred after the formation of Partnerships British Columbia. See page ii.

4. U.S. Department of Transportation, *Report to Congress on Public-Private Partnerships*, December 2004, 42, http://www.fhwa.dot.gov/reports/pppdec2004/pppdec2004 (accessed August 5, 2009).

5. Jose A. Gomez-Ibanez and John R. Meyer, *Going Private: The International Experience with Road Privatization* (Washington, DC: Brookings Institution, 1993), 142.

6. U.S. Department of Transportation, Federal Highway Administration, *Public-Private Partnerships for Highway Infrastructure: Capitalizing on International Experience*, 2009, 3, http://international.fhwa.dot.gov/pubs/pl09010/ pl09010.pdf (accessed September 1, 2009).

7. Ibid.

8. Ibid.

9. Robert W. Poole and Peter Samuel, *Pennsylvania Turnpike Alternatives: A Review and Critique of the Democratic Caucus Study*, Reason Foundation Policy Brief 70, April 2008, 5, http://reason.org/files/cd52022e2d52ff1d17fd6423645c6642.pdf (accessed September 7, 2009).

10. Ibid.

11. Gunter J. Zeitlow, "Role of the Private Sector in Managing and Maintaining Roads," in *Street Smart: Competition, Entrepreneurship, and the Future of Roads*, ed. Gabriel Roth (New Brunswick, NJ: Transaction Publishers, 2006). This discussion relies on the findings reported therein.

12. In March 2010, Transfield, in a partnership with Dexter Construction Company, won a 30-year road maintenance and rehabilitation contract in Canada. See AAP, "Transfield Wins Canadian Road Contract," *Sydney Morning Herald*, March 15, 2010.

13. Christina Malmberg Calvo and Sven Ivarsson, "Private Roads to the Future: The Swedish Private Road Associations," in *Street Smart: Competition, Entrepreneurship, and the Future of Roads*, ed. Gabriel Roth (New Brunswick, NJ: Transaction Publishers, 2006), 327–46.

14. See, for example, Aidan R. Vining and Anthony E. Boardman, "Ownership versus Competition: Efficiency in Public Enterprise," *Public Choice* 73 (1992): 205–39.

15. DLA Piper, *European PPP Report 2007*, http://www.irfnet.ch/files-upload/knowledges/DLAPiper_European-PPP-Report2007.pdf (accessed April 2, 2010).

16. Statistics are from Peter Samuel, "The Way Forward to the Private Provision of Public Roads," in *Street Smart: Competition, Entrepreneurship, and the Future of Roads*, ed. Gabriel Roth (New Brunswick, NJ: Transaction Publishers, 2006), 501–30. Autostrade is a privately owned, publicly traded company that emerged out of the subsequently privatized state-owned enterprise that constructed many Italian roads in the postwar period.

17. These are typically BOOT contracts. See the articles in "Policy Forum: Financing Public Infrastructure," *Australian Economic Review* 38, no. 4 (2005), from which this discussion borrows.

18. Christine Brown, "Financing Transport Infrastructure: For Whom the Road Tolls," *Australian Economic Review* 38, no. 4 (2005): 431–38.

19. U.S. Department of Transportation, Federal Highway Administration, *Case Studies of Transportation: Public-Private Partnerships around the World*, July 7, 2007, 4–7, http://www.fhwa.dot.gov/PPP/pdf/int_ppp_case_studies_finalreport_7-7-07.pdf (accessed August 10, 2009). Later Sydney PPP projects incorporated more equal risk-sharing arrangements.

20. New South Wales Treasury, Office of Financial Management, Research and Information, "NSW Public-Private Partnerships Policy—An Evolution," March 2009, 4.

21. See Demi Chung, "Private Provision of Transport Infrastructure—Unveiling the Inconvenient Truth in New South Wales" (31st Australasia Transport Research Forum, Queensland, Australia, October 3, 2008), 15.

22. Demi Chung, *Public-Private Partnerships: A Prudent Fiscal Approach to Foster Capital Accumulation.*

23. Deloitte Consulting, *Closing the Infrastructure Gap: The Role of Public-Private Partnerships*, 2006, 9, http://www.deloitte.com/dtt/cda/doc/content/us_ps_Closing InfrastructureGap2006(1).pdf (accessed September 9, 2010).

24. See Allen Consulting Group, *Performance of PPPs and Traditional Procurement in Australia, Final Report*, November 30, 2007, http://www.ippp.org/TheAllen Group.pdf (accessed November 25, 2008), from which this discussion borrows.

25. For a detailed discussion, see David Czerwinski and R. Richard Geddes, "Policy Issues in U.S. Transportation Public-Private Partnerships: Lessons from Australia," research report prepared for the Mineta Transportation Institute, forthcoming 2011.

26. Bob Carr, "Good Roads Sooner: Public-Private Partnerships in New South Wales," in *Innovators in Action 2009*, Reason Foundation, January 29, 2010, http://reason.org/news/show/good-roads-sooner-public-priva (accessed February 24, 2010). Similarly, the Federal Highway Administration in its scanning study notes that "Australian states have used highway PPPs selectively in their urban centers to implement large-scale surface mobility improvements in a relatively short timeframe. These highways have improved both commuter and freight travel in the most densely populated cities in Australia—Sydney, Melbourne, and Brisbane. Similar to Spain, the activity in Australia has spawned an industry of highway developers, operators, and financiers. These private firms are also positioned to provide their services across the globe." U.S. Department of Transportation, Federal Highway Administration, *Public-Private Partnerships for Highway Infrastructure*, 49.

27. See Matthieu Desiderio, *Public-Private Partnerships, French Practices and Evolutions*, Transport Expertise Association, February 26, 2008, http://en.transport-expertise.org/index.php/2008/02/26/public-private-partnerships-french-practices-and-evolutions (accessed September 3, 2009).

28. Ibid., 3.

29. Ibid., 4.

30. Peter Samuel, "Japan's Tollster 'Privatization' Proceeds but Government Falls over Postal Divestiture," *TOLLROADSnews*, August 10, 2005, http://www.tollroadsnews.com/node/1212 (accessed December 5, 2008).

31. Germá Bel and Xavier Fageda, "Is a Mixed Funding Model for the Highway Network Sustainable Over Time? The Spanish Case," in *Procurement and Financing of Motorways in Europe*, ed. G. Ragazzi and W. Rothengatter (Oxford: Elsevier,

2005), 195–211; and U.S. Department of Transportation, Federal Highway Administration, *Public-Private Partnerships for Highway Infrastructure*, 9.

32. Germá Bel and Xavier Fageda, "Is a Mixed Funding Model," 203.

33. See chapter 2.

34. U.S. Department of Transportation, Federal Highway Administration, *Public-Private Partnerships for Highway Infrastructure*, 20.

35. Ibid., 47.

36. The Carnation Revolution, a left-leaning revolution in which four people were killed by government forces, occurred in April 1974. It replaced a fascist dictatorship with a democratic government. See Knowledgerush, s.v. "Carnation Revolution," http://www.knowledgerush.com/kr/encyclopedia/Carnation_Revolution (accessed April 2, 2010).

37. U.S. Department of Transportation, Federal Highway Administration, *Public-Private Partnerships for Highway Infrastructure*, 9.

38. Peter Samuel, "Portugal to Toll All Motorways," *TOLLROADSnews*, November 13, 2004, http://www.tollroadsnews.com/node/889 (accessed August 5, 2009).

39. U.S. Department of Transportation, Federal Highway Administration, *Public-Private Partnerships for Highway Infrastructure*, 19.

40. Ibid.

41. Ibid., 21.

42. See U.S. Department of Transportation, Federal Highway Administration, *Case Studies of Transportation*, from which this discussion borrows.

43. UK Department for Transport, Highways Agency, "About DBFOs: History and Objectives," http://www.highways.gov.uk/roads/3008.aspx (accessed August 10, 2009).

44. Ibid.

45. U.S. Department of Transportation, Federal Highway Administration, *Case Studies of Transportation*, 3-3.

46. Ibid., 22.

Chapter 8: Public-Private Partnerships in the Public Interest

1. U.S. Department of Transportation, Federal Highway Administration, *Public Policy Considerations in Public-Private Partnerships (PPP) Arrangements*, January 2009, http://www.fhwa.dot.gov/PPP/pdf/2009_public_policy_considerations_ppp_arrangements.pdf (accessed September 3, 2009); Jeffrey N. Buxbaum and Iris N. Ortiz, *Protecting the Public Interest: The Role of Long-Term Concession Agreements for Providing Transportation Infrastructure*, USC Keston Institute for Public Finance and Infrastructure Policy, Research Paper 07-02, June 2007, http://www.uscedu/schools/sppd/keston/pdf/20070618-trans-concession-agreements.pdf (accessed April 5, 2010); and Jeffrey N. Buxbaum and Iris N. Ortiz, *Public Sector Decision Making for Public-Private Partnerships: A Synthesis of Highway Practice*, Transportation Research Board, National Cooperative Highway Research Program,

NCHRP Synthesis 391, 2009, http://onlinepubs.trb.org/onlinepubs/nchrp/nchrp_syn_391.pdf (accessed September 3, 2009).

2. See chapter 5 for a discussion of issues clarified by state PPP-enabling legislation.

3. Pew Center on the States, *Driven by Dollars: What States Should Know When Considering Public-Private Partnerships to Fund Transportation*, 2009, 2, http://www.pewtrusts.org/uploadedFiles/wwwpewtrustsorg/Reports/State_policy/PA_Turnpike_FINAL_WEB.pdf (accessed September 2, 2009).

4. See Partnerships British Columbia, "About Us," http://www.partnershipsbc.ca.files/about.html (accessed August 6, 2009).

5. See Partnerships Victoria, "About Partnerships Victoria," http://www.partnerships.vic.gov.au (accessed August 6, 2009).

6. According to a Federal Highway Administration study of PPPs in several countries, "All public agencies [emphasize] the need for transparency during the procurement process for PPP projects. The typical scale and complexity of PPP highway projects generate an unusually high level of public, political, and media attention. Nearly all of the agencies visited go to substantial lengths to make project documents and records accessible. In addition, some agencies use a public auditor to monitor proceedings." U.S. Department of Transportation, Federal Highway Administration, *Public-Private Partnerships for Highway Infrastructure: Capitalizing on International Experience*, 2009, 3, http://international.fhwa.dot.gov/pubs/pl09010/pl09010.pdf (accessed September 1, 2009).

7. See Eduardo M. R. A. Engel, Ronald Fischer, and Alexander Galetovic, "Privatizing Highways in the United States," *Review of Industrial Organization* 29, no. 1 (2006): 27–53; and Eduardo M. R. A. Engel, Ronald Fischer, and Alexander Galetovic, "Least-Present-Value-of-Revenue Auctions and Highway Franchising," *Journal of Political Economy* 109, no. 5 (2001): 993–1020.

8. Eduardo M. R. A. Engel, Ronald Fischer, and Alexander Galetovic, "Privatizing Highways in the United States," 38.

9. See Pew Center on the States, *Driven by Dollars*, 10–14.

10. Ibid., 11–13.

11. Performance measures in lease agreements are often based on levels of service defined in state highway design manuals, which focus on traffic flows and motorists' experience in using the facility. See Pew Center on the States, *Driven by Dollars*, 32. For an example of a state highway design manual, see California Department of Transportation, *Highway Design Manual*, http://www.dot.ca.gov/hq/oppd/hdm/hdmtoc.htm (accessed April 5, 2010).

12. Leonard C. Gilroy, "Politicizing Privatization Isn't in Taxpayers' Best Interest," Reason Foundation, August 27, 2008, http://reason.org/news/show/politicizing-privatization-isn (accessed September 5, 2010).

13. In economic terms, setting price above incremental cost results in the value of facility use to the last vehicle, or marginal benefit, exceeding its cost, which generates a deadweight or social loss.

14. Some PPP contracts, such as that on the 407 Express Toll Route in Canada, as discussed below, have focused on regulating traffic volumes rather than on the toll itself, which would help address this problem.

15. A large literature supports this view. See, for example, Emeka T. Nwaeze, "Rate-of-Return Regulation and the Behavior of the Return on Equity for Electric Utilities," *Journal of Economics and Business* 49, no. 5 (1997): 491–510; and W. Kip Viscusi, Joseph E. Harrington, and John M. Vernon, "Introduction," in *Economics of Regulation and Antitrust*, 4th ed. (Cambridge, MA: MIT Press, 2005).

16. A firm receives a normal rate of return when its inputs are just earning their opportunity cost—that is, when they are currently earning what they could in their next-best alternative use, whatever that may be. Economically, a simple way of relating a firm's pricing power to the degree of competition (that is, available alternatives) is through the Lerner Index. The Lerner Index (also called the price markup) for product i is defined as $\dfrac{P_i - MC_i}{P_i} = -\dfrac{1}{\varepsilon_i}$ where MC_i is marginal cost, which is how cost varies with output of product i (mathematically $\dfrac{\partial C_i}{\partial Q_i}$) and ε_i is the elasticity of demand for product i (mathematically $\varepsilon_i = \dfrac{\Delta Q_i}{\Delta P_i}\dfrac{P_i}{Q_i}$). As the number of substitutes for product i rises (that is, it faces more competition), then the elasticity of demand for i also rises, and the firm's pricing power declines.

17. Economically, such actions and alternative modes will increase the elasticity of demand, or ε_i, where i is the service provided by I-95. They in turn reduce I-95's Lerner Index. Scholars have recognized that roads will often face competition. De Palma and Lindsey, for example, state that "in addressing this task it is important to recognize that private roads will typically face competition from other roads. One reason is simply that alternative routes often exist between given origins and destinations." See André de Palma and Robin Lindsey, "Private Roads, Competition, and Incentives to Adopt Time-Based Congestion Tolling," *Journal of Urban Economics* 52 (2002): 218.

18. See David E. M. Sappington, "Price Regulation," in *Structure, Regulation, and Competition*, ed. M. Cave, S. Majumdar, and I. Vogelsang (Oxford: Elsevier Science Publishers, 2002), 225–93. This terminology is now widely accepted, but it is somewhat misleading, since RORR also creates meaningful incentives for the firm. For a discussion of the differences between price-cap regulation and RORR, see Michael E. Beesley and Stephen C. Littlechild, "The Regulation of Privatized Monopolies in the United Kingdom," *Rand Journal of Economics* 20, no. 3 (1989): 454–72.

19. See David E. M. Sappington, "Price Regulation," 240–43, for a summary of the critiques of RORR.

20. Viscusi et al., *Economics of Regulation and Antitrust*, 503.

21. Harvey Averch and Leland L. Johnson, "Behavior of the Firm under Regulatory Constraint," *American Economic Review* 52 (1962): 1052–69. See also Ronald J. Daniels and Michael J. Trebilcock, "Private Provision of Public Infrastructure: An Organizational Analysis of the Next Privatization Frontier," *University of Toronto Law Review* 46, no. 3 (1996): 392.

22. Legislative Study Committee on Private Participation in Toll Roads, *Report of the Legislative Study Committee on Private Participation in Toll Projects,* 2008, 61, ftp://ftp.dot.state.tx.us/pub/txdot-info/library/pubs/bus/tta/sb_792_report.pdf (accessed September 2, 2009).

23. U.S. Government Accountability Office, *Highway Public-Private Partnerships: More Rigorous Up-front Analysis Could Better Secure Potential Benefits and Protect the Public Interest,* GAO-08-44, 2008, 26, http://www.gao.gov/new.items/ d0844.pdf (accessed September 1, 2009).

24. For further discussion, see David E. M. Sappington, "Price Regulation," 241.

25. See ibid., 231.

26. Darrin Grimsey and Mervyn K. Lewis, "Evaluating the Risks of Public Private Partnerships for Infrastructure Projects," *International Journal of Project Management* 20, no. 2 (2002): 108.

27. See Legislative Study Committee on Private Participation in Toll Roads, *Report of the Legislative Study Committee,* 61.

28. Peter Samuel, *Should States Sell Their Toll Roads?* Reason Foundation Policy Study 334, June 2, 2005, 6–7, http://reason.org/news/show/12767.htm (accessed September 1, 2009).

29. See chapter 2.

30. National Surface Transportation Infrastructure Financing Commission, *Paying Our Way: A New Framework for Transportation Finance,* February 2009, 179, http://financecommission.dot.gov/Documents/NSTIF_Commission_Final_Report_Mar09FNL.pdf (accessed February 5, 2010).

31. Interestingly, the Chicago Skyway concession did not contain a noncompete clause because geographical constraints make the building of competing roadways very costly.

32. See Czerwinski and Geddes, "Policy Issues in U.S. Transportation."

33. Peter Samuel, *The Role of Tolls in Financing 21st Century Highways,* Reason Foundation Policy Study 359, 2007, 36.

34. See Legislative Study Committee on Private Participation in Toll Roads, *Report of the Legislative Study Committee,* 56.

35. This discussion borrows from Erik Sanzenbach, "U.S. 11 Bridge Celebrates 80th Birthday," *St. Tammany News,* February 18, 2008, http://www.newsbanner.com/articles/2008/02/18/news/news02.txt (accessed December 1, 2008).

36. U.S. Government Accountability Office, *Highway Public-Private Partnerships: More Rigorous Up-front Analysis,* 11.

37. For an example of noncompete clauses in airport construction, see Ronald J. Daniels and Michael J. Trebilcock, "Private Provision," 385.

38. Ibid., 383.

39. Indeed, anticipated use of concession proceeds was identified as another key reason for the failure of the proposed lease of the Pennsylvania Turnpike. See Pew Center on the States, *Driven by Dollars*, 2–3, which identifies disagreements about returns on proceed investment, the plan for proceed investment, and oversight of proceed spending as key factors in undermining the lease.

40. See chapter 3.

41. See Michael C. Jensen, "Takeovers: Their Causes and Consequences," *Journal of Economic Perspectives* 2, no. 1 (Winter 1988): 21–48. For a technical accounting definition, see Investopedia, s.v. "Free Cash Flow-FPF," http://www.investopedia.com/terms/f/freecashflow.asp (accessed April 5, 2010).

42. Michael C. Jensen, "Takeovers: Their Causes and Consequences," 28–29.

43. The Alaska Permanent Fund is in the spirit of a dividend payout. See Wikipedia, s.v. "Permanent Fund," http://en.wikipedia.org/wiki/Alaska_ Permanent_ Fund (accessed April 6, 2010).

44. See chapter 2.

45. U.S. Department of Transportation, Federal Highway Administration, *Public Policy Considerations*, 18. See especially table 5.1.

46. See Wikipedia, s.v. "Project Financing," http://en.wikipedia.org/wiki/ Project_financing (accessed April 6, 2010).

47. For a detailed discussion of the special problems arising from government as a contracting partner in the provision of infrastructure, see Ronald J. Daniels and Michael J. Trebilcock, "Private Provision," 412–19.

48. See, for example, Ronald M. Harstad and Michael A. Crew, "Franchise Bidding without Holdups: Utility Regulation with Efficient Pricing and Choice of Provider," *Journal of Regulatory Economics* 15 (1999): 141–63; and Keith J. Crocker and Scott E. Masten, "Regulation and Administered Contracts Revisited: Lessons from Transaction-Cost Economics for Public Utility Regulation," *Journal of Regulatory Economics* 9 (1996): 5–39.

49. See Peter Samuel, *The Role of Tolls*, 38.

50. See David Czerwinski and R. Richard Geddes, "Policy Issues in U.S. Transportation."

51. U.S. Department of Transportation, Federal Highway Administration, *Public-Private Partnerships for Highway Infrastructure*, 3.

52. Ibid.

53. Ibid.

54. See Robert Poole, "Learning from Abroad: Highway PPPs Overseas," *Surface Transportation Innovations* 68, Reason Foundation, June 11, 200 9, http://reason.org/news/show/surface-transportation-innovat-68 (accessed August 17, 2009).

Index

About the Author

R. Richard Geddes is associate professor in the Department of Policy Analysis and Management at Cornell University. In addition to his teaching and research at Cornell, Professor Geddes served as a commissioner on the National Surface Transportation Policy and Revenue Study Commission, which submitted its report to the U.S. Congress in January 2008. He is also a Mineta Transportation Institute research associate. In 2009, he served as a Fulbright Senior Scholar at Australian National University, and in 2010 as a visiting researcher at the Australian government's Productivity Commission, studying transportation public-private partnerships in Australia. He has held positions as a senior economist on the Council of Economic Advisers, as a visiting faculty fellow at Yale Law School, and as a national fellow at the Hoover Institution at Stanford University. He received his PhD in economics from the University of Chicago in 1991, and his bachelor's degree in economics and finance from Towson State University in 1984.

Jeremy A. Rabkin
Professor of Law
George Mason University
School of Law

Richard J. Zeckhauser
Frank Plumpton Ramsey Professor
of Political Economy
Kennedy School of Government
Harvard University

Research Staff

Ali Alfoneh
Resident Fellow

Joseph Antos
Wilson H. Taylor Scholar in Health
Care and Retirement Policy

Leon Aron
Resident Scholar; Director,
Russian Studies

Paul S. Atkins
Visiting Scholar

Michael Auslin
Resident Scholar

Claude Barfield
Resident Scholar

Michael Barone
Resident Fellow

Roger Bate
Legatum Fellow in Global Prosperity

Walter Berns
Resident Scholar

Andrew G. Biggs
Resident Scholar

Edward Blum
Visiting Fellow

Dan Blumenthal
Resident Fellow

John R. Bolton
Senior Fellow

Karlyn Bowman
Senior Fellow

Alex Brill
Research Fellow

John E. Calfee
Resident Scholar

Charles W. Calomiris
Visiting Scholar

Lynne V. Cheney
Senior Fellow

Steven J. Davis
Visiting Scholar

Mauro De Lorenzo
Visiting Fellow

Christopher DeMuth
D. C. Searle Senior Fellow

Thomas Donnelly
Resident Fellow; Director,
AEI Center for Defense Studies

Nicholas Eberstadt
Henry Wendt Scholar in
Political Economy

Jon Entine
Visiting Fellow

John C. Fortier
Research Fellow

Newt Gingrich
Senior Fellow

Jonah Goldberg
Visiting Fellow

Scott Gottlieb, M.D.
Resident Fellow

Kenneth P. Green
Resident Scholar

Michael S. Greve
John G. Searle Scholar

Kevin A. Hassett
Senior Fellow; Director,
Economic Policy Studies

Steven F. Hayward
F. K. Weyerhaeuser Fellow

Robert B. Helms
Resident Scholar

Arthur Herman
NRI Visiting Scholar

Frederick M. Hess
Resident Scholar; Director,
Education Policy Studies

Ayaan Hirsi Ali
Resident Fellow

R. Glenn Hubbard
Visiting Scholar

Frederick W. Kagan
Resident Scholar; Director,
AEI Critical Threats Project

Leon R. Kass, M.D.
Madden-Jewett Chair

Andrew P. Kelly
Research Fellow

Desmond Lachman
Resident Fellow

Adam Lerrick
Visiting Scholar

Philip I. Levy
Resident Scholar

Lawrence B. Lindsey
Visiting Scholar

John H. Makin
Resident Scholar

Aparna Mathur
Resident Scholar

Lawrence M. Mead
Visiting Scholar

Allan H. Meltzer
Visiting Scholar

Thomas P. Miller
Resident Fellow

Charles Murray
W. H. Brady Scholar

Roger F. Noriega
Visiting Fellow

Michael Novak
George Frederick Jewett Scholar
in Religion, Philosophy, and
Public Policy

Norman J. Ornstein
Resident Scholar

Richard Perle
Resident Fellow

Mark J. Perry
Visiting Scholar

Tomas J. Philipson
Visiting Scholar

Edward Pinto
Resident Fellow

Alex J. Pollock
Resident Fellow

Vincent R. Reinhart
Resident Scholar

Michael Rubin
Resident Scholar

Sally Satel, M.D.
Resident Scholar

Gary J. Schmitt
Resident Scholar; Director,
Program on American Citizenship

Mark Schneider
Visiting Scholar

David Schoenbrod
Visiting Scholar

Nick Schulz
DeWitt Wallace Fellow;
Editor-in-Chief, American.com

Roger Scruton
Visiting Scholar

Apoorva Shah
Research Fellow

Kent Smetters
Visiting Scholar

Christina Hoff Sommers
Resident Scholar; Director,
W. H. Brady Program

Tim Sullivan
Research Fellow

Phillip Swagel
Visiting Scholar

Erin Syron
NRI Fellow

Marc A. Thiessen
Visiting Fellow

Bill Thomas
Visiting Fellow

Alan D. Viard
Resident Scholar

Peter J. Wallison
Arthur F. Burns Fellow in
Financial Policy Studies

David A. Weisbach
Visiting Scholar

Paul Wolfowitz
Visiting Scholar

John Yoo
Visiting Scholar

Benjamin Zycher
NRI Visiting Fellow